T0330246

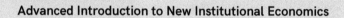

Advanced Introduction to New Institutional Economics

Elgar Advanced Introductions are stimulating and thoughtful introductions to major fields in the social sciences, business and law, expertly written by the world's leading scholars. Designed to be accessible yet rigorous, they offer concise and lucid surveys of the substantive and policy issues associated with discrete subject areas.

The aims of the series are two-fold: to pinpoint essential principles of a particular field, and to offer insights that stimulate critical thinking. By distilling the vast and often technical corpus of information on the subject into a concise and meaningful form, the books serve as accessible introductions for undergraduate and graduate students coming to the subject for the first time. Importantly, they also develop well-informed, nuanced critiques of the field that will challenge and extend the understanding of advanced students, scholars and policy-makers.

For a full list of titles in the series please see the back of the book. Recent titles in the series include:

Advanced Introduction to

New Institutional Economics

CLAUDE MÉNARD

Professor of Economics, Centre d'Economie de la Sorbonne, Université de Paris (Panthéon-Sorbonne), France

MARY M. SHIRLEY

President, Ronald Coase Institute, USA

Elgar Advanced Introductions

 Edward Elgar
PUBLISHING

Cheltenham, UK • Northampton, MA, USA

Published by
Edward Elgar Publishing Limited
The Lypiatts
15 Lansdown Road
Cheltenham
Glos GL50 2JA
UK

Edward Elgar Publishing, Inc.
William Pratt House
9 Dewey Court
Northampton
Massachusetts 01060
USA

A catalogue record for this book
is available from the British Library

Library of Congress Control Number: 2021949016

ISBN 978 1 78990 448 2 (cased)
ISBN 978 1 78990 450 5 (paperback)
ISBN 978 1 78990 449 9 (eBook)

Printed and bound in Great Britain by TJ Books Limited, Padstow, Cornwall

Contents

Figures and table

FIGURES

TABLE

Boxes

Preface

In the decades since its beginning in the early 1970s, new institutional economics (NIE) has begun transforming economics, as Ronald Coase once predicted. "This change will not come about, in my view, as a result of a frontal assault on mainstream economics. It will come as a result of economists in branches or subsections of economics adopting a different approach, as indeed is already happening." And in the end, "all of economics will have become what we now call 'the new institutional economics'" (Coase, 1998a: 73–4). Beyond economics, NIE has also deeply influenced political science, management, law, and sociology. This success is a product of NIE's usefulness for understanding real world phenomena through its trademark combination of theoretical concepts rooted in a concrete vision of reality with an emphasis on empirical testing using a variety of methods. Thanks to its dynamism, realism, and utility, NIE has generated a rich research agenda which has begun changing the nature of the intellectual and policy debates.

NIE encompasses a diverse set of ideas unified around a shared belief in the central role of institutions, transaction costs, property rights, and contracts. From this strong central trunk, NIE developed branches focusing on the fundamental institutional environment, the governance of transactions and organizations, and the role of communal organizations and collective action. This arborescence, while frustrating to those who prefer a more disciplined and contained theory, is also a secret of NIE's success, allowing the dynamism and diversity that keep it on the frontiers of knowledge. NIE has been particularly successful in addressing questions about the organization of economies (e.g., Why choose firms vs. markets vs. alternative arrangements? Why make or buy? Which contract for which transaction?); the development of states and societies (e.g., Why rich or poor? When and why do modern state and legal systems emerge?

Why do deficient institutions persist?); and issues surrounding property and the environment (e.g., When are shared resources overexploited? What incentives emerge from which property rights? How do communities overcome their collective action problems to manage communal resources?).

This book begins with an overview of the basics of NIE (Chapter 1) and an analysis of each of its three shared concepts: transaction costs (Chapter 2), property rights (Chapter 3), and contracts (Chapter 4). From this trunk we turn to the branches: first, organizations (Chapter 5), a preoccupation of the branch associated with Oliver Williamson, and states and legal systems (Chapter 6), a focus of the Northian branch. We follow this with two chapters on themes that cut across NIE, the making of public policy (Chapter 7) and institutional change and development (Chapter 8), and conclude with a brief consideration of the future of NIE (Chapter 9).

As befits an introduction, we have concentrated on the shared concepts and approaches that make NIE distinctive. Along the way, we point out some important divergences, but our focus is predominantly on the areas of agreement rather than of controversy. The extensive references provided along our journey allow interested readers to dive deeper into specific topics.

The material we synthesize in this 'advanced introduction' builds on years of teaching at various universities; organizing workshops, particularly within the Ronald Coase Institute; researching and publishing on institutional issues; and organizing or participating in numerous international conferences. Although we assume full responsibility for its content (and possible misinterpretations), the book benefited from extensive feedback. More specifically, we owe much to Terry Anderson, Lee Benham, Elodie Bertrand, Sandro Cabral, Jean Ensminger, Robert Gibbons, Christopher Hartwell, P.J. Hill, Gary Libecap, Camille Limoges, Dean Lueck, Joanne Oxley, Emmanuel Raynaud, Syvia Saes, Stéphane Saussier, Valentin Seidler, Andrey Shastitko, Colin Xu, and Giorgio Zanarone who generously provided comments on specific chapters or segments of this book. Jonathan Greenacre and Phil Keefer deserve special thanks for their careful review and comments on several chapters.

1   Building a new paradigm

New institutional economics (NIE) is not a single theory, but a dynamic tree with branches growing from a strong trunk of shared fundamental concepts. The most basic shared concept is that institutions – humanly devised rules and norms – are crucial to understanding the organization and workings of economies and societies. We start this chapter with the trunk: what are institutions and why do they exist? What are the core concepts shared by new institutionalists (Section 1.1)? Next, we consider the branches: ideas from Ronald Coase's original insights that were expanded and developed by a small group of leading scholars rooted in a rich intellectual tradition into different but complementary research agendas (1.2). Finally, we consider the assumptions and methodology of NIE and how they are both somewhat similar to and different from the neoclassical model[1] (1.3), as well as game theory and old institutional economics (1.4).

1.1   Core concepts: the trunk of NIE

1.1.1   What are institutions?

While diverse in their definitions, NIE authors are united in their commitment to restoring institutions to the core of economic analysis. The most widely used definition is that of Douglass North: "Institutions are the rules of the game in a society," which define "the framework within which human interaction takes place" (1990a: 3, 4). North illustrated this

---

[1]   In this book, we use the term "neo-classical" to refer to approaches focusing on the role of the price mechanism to transfer goods and services through markets. The resulting models are centered on partial equilibrium, with exchanges on specific markets, and general equilibrium, with consideration for interdependent markets. These models are at the core of most economic textbooks.

through the example of professional football. In professional football, as in other sports,

> The game is played within a set of formal rules, informal norms (such as not deliberately injuring a key player on the opposing team), and the use of referees and umpires to enforce the rules and norms. How the game is actually played depends not only on the formal rules and informal norms that define the incentive structure for the players, but also on the effectiveness of enforcement of the rules and norms. Changing the formal rules will alter the way the game is played but also, as anyone who has watched professional football knows, it frequently pays to evade the rules and norms (and deliberately injure the quarterback of the opposing team). So it is with the performance characteristics of an economy. (North, 2005: 48; also 1990a: 4)

Although numerous variations on this definition have been proposed (Ostrom, 1996; 2014; Williamson, 1996; 2000; Furubotn and Richter, 1997; Greif, 2006; Hodgson, 2015; Alston et al., 2018; Kunneke, Menard and Groenewegen, 2021, to name but a few), North's has stood the test of numerous empirical applications and for that reason we stick to the Northian perspective in this book.

1.1.2   Institutional layers

As the professional football example suggests, not all rules are the same. Specific types of rules define different institutional layers. North distinguished between the institutional environment and organizations. The institutional environment refers to "the set of fundamental political, social, and legal ground rules that establishes the basis for production, exchange, and distribution. Rules governing elections, property rights, and the right of contract are examples of the type of ground rules that make up the economic environment" (Davis and North, 1971: 6). "Organizations consist of specific groups of individuals pursuing a mix of common and individual goals … Organizations coordinate their members' actions, so an organization's actions are more than the sum of the actions of the individuals" (North, Wallis and Weingast, 2009: 15). Most organizations have their own internal institutional structure that influences the way members behave towards one another and towards non-members.[2] This distinction between institutions and organizations

---

[2]   Greif (2006) saw organizations as both components of institutions and as institutions in their own right, while North considered institutions as the rules of the game and organizations as the players of the game.

delineates the two main branches of NIE: one focuses on the fundamental ground rules of the institutional environment, often identified as the "Northian" branch, and the other on organizations and their governing institutions, or the "Williamsonian" branch.

Considerable research has enriched the initial framework by introducing additional layers of rules composing the institutional environment (e.g., Weingast and Marshall, 1988; Williamson, 2000; Ostrom, 2005; 2014; Alston et al., 2018; Kunneke, Menard and Groenewegen, 2021), although dividing lines and terminology vary. Box 1.1 gives an empirical example of institutional layers.

Box 1.1   Institutional layers illustrated

The origin of the idea that institutions involve different layers can be traced to several analyses by Ronald Coase of "public utilities." His article on how the British Broadcasting Corporation (BBC) was born is a good example (Coase, 1947).

Wireless telephone, as radio broadcasting was called at the time, was regulated in Great Britain under the Wireless Telegraphy Act of 1904. The Act considered radio transmission to be a means for sending messages in situations in which wire telephone was not available (typically aboard ships). In the early 1920s, the Marconi Company started emitting radio programs in Great Britain on a very modest scale. To expand an activity that was still largely experimental, Marconi needed a license from the British Post Office, the regulator in charge of implementing the 1904 law. However, the Post Office was reluctant to issue a license, since it did not have a good understanding of the emerging technology and was suspicious about the potential of transmitting news and commentaries through radio broadcasting. Marconi and other companies pressured the Post Office to award extended broadcasting rights, and after two years of arduous negotiations among the interested firms and with the Post Office, with the Post Office pushing firms to cooperate, the BBC was created with a monopoly over broadcasting. The capital of the new organization was initially in the hands of the participating firms, which operated under tight regulation by the Post Office. For example, all components of 'receiving sets' had to be produced in Great Britain. Coase clearly identified the different layers involved in this story: (1) the legal framework, (2) a regulatory agency (the British Post

Office), and (3) the operating organization – the BBC (more details in Menard, 2016: 188).

North (1990a) portrays what we might call a "macro" layer of institutions, a complex of rules and norms that frame the "institutional environment" and determine the security of property rights, enforcement of contracts, efficiency and impartiality of judicial systems, and incentives and capacity of state actors to protect order and provide broad-based public goods, control violence and curb the abuse of power, and so on. North suggests a hierarchy of formal rules with narrowly defined regulations and laws at the bottom and fundamental laws such as constitutions at the top, where each level is more costly to change than the previous level. Formal rules are given stability by supportive informal institutions, which "have tenacious survival ability because they have become part of habitual behavior" (83). The "micro" layer contains the rules and norms operating within what Williamson identified as organizations as well as framing agreements between organizations. Micro institutions determine how transactions are organized (the choice between markets, firms or hybrids[3]), the division of labor, the incentives to produce and invest, and so on. These institutions change frequently and their changes sometimes have cumulative effects on macro institutions. Building on insights from North, Williamson, Ostrom, and others, some scholars (e.g., Menard, 2014, 2017; Kunneke, Menard and Groenewegen, 2021: ch. 2) have suggested an intermediate or "meso" layer – the layer containing domain-specific regulations and norms that operate between the fundamental governmental and societal rules in the macro layer and the rules governing organizations and markets in the micro layer. Meso institutions adapt the macro rules to specific domains (e.g., directives adapting a law on public-private partnerships to a specific sector or location). Meso organizations operate as intermediaries, implementing and enforcing the rules of the game and providing feedback that influences policy makers. Examples are regulatory agencies and bureaus, arbitration boards, patent agencies, certifying and standardizing organizations, and the like.

---

[3]   "Hybrids" in the Williamsonian approach are inter-organizational structures, such as joint ventures or franchising (see Chapter 5).

1.1.3   Formal rules, informal/social norms, and beliefs

Besides layers, the NIE literature distinguishes between what North called formal and informal institutions, although again terminology and dividing lines differ. The concept of formal institutions is straightforward. They are codified, traceable, and transmissible rules, usually written, and enforced by organized third parties such as state legal systems or private arbitration courts. The Hammurabi code, the French Declaration of Rights, the US Constitution, laws regarding property rights, or corporate laws are all examples (Kunneke, Menard and Groenewegen, 2021: ch. 2). North (1990a: ch. 6) also includes more specific rules such as bylaws and contractual regimes.

Informal institutions are interpreted in a variety of ways.[4] In this book, we follow North (1990a), who called them unwritten codes of conduct that arise to coordinate repeated human interaction. (See Box 1.2 for an example.) Ostrom (2014: 10) described norms as "preferences related to prescriptions about actions or outcomes that are not focused primarily on short-term material payoffs to self." While rules for Ostrom (2014) require some sort of monitoring and sanctioning mechanism, norms are acquired as part of a community and have an internal value that is strongly reinforced when the community might observe rule-breaking.

North described three kinds of informal rules and norms: (1) extensions, elaborations, and modifications of formal rules (such as the unwritten constraints that govern US congressional committees); (2) socially sanctioned norms of behavior (such as social pressures for fair trading, civic duty, or duels of honor); and (3) internally enforced standards of conduct (such as self-commitment to honesty or similar values). North (1990a) views these informal rules and norms as part of "culture," another confusing term, which North defines as do Boyd and Richerson (1985: 2) as "the

---

[4]   For example, Alston et al. (2018) define institutions as deliberately constructed. In this view, norms are not institutions since they arise from repeated behavior, a spontaneous order. In contrast, Greif (2006: 30) argues that institutions include beliefs, as well as norms, rules and organizations because together they generate a (social) regularity of behavior that is self-enforcing. If there is no behavioral regularity, there is no institution. To Voigt (2019) only state enforced rules are formal, while informal (or "internal") institutions include private rules such as contracts enforced by private arbitration.

transmission from one generation to the next, via teaching and imitation, of knowledge, values and other factors that influence behavior." (For more on culture, see Chapter 8: 8.5.) To North informal institutions primarily reflect a society's dominant beliefs ("the beliefs of those in a position to make the rules of the game") and may evolve over time but "are not typically amenable to deliberate human manipulation" (North, 2005: 50). Some informal rules are so ingrained as to be self-enforced, while others are socially sanctioned through the threat of loss of reputation and social ostracism (see Bernstein, 1992 or Aoki, 2001 for examples).

Despite the disparity in how new institutionalists define informal institutions, there is broad agreement that humanly designed, unwritten rules shape behavior, persist over time, and are enforced by society or have been so internalized by individuals as to be self-enforcing. Allen points out that many institutions that seem strange to us might have been designed to solve incentive problems that arose in different circumstances when they served "to generate wealth through reduced shirking, pilfering, embezzlement, theft, dereliction of duty, cowardice and the host of other bad behaviors that arise when people come together ..." (Allen, 2012: 14).

Box 1.2   Informal rules and networks

Avner Greif (1993; 1994; 2006) provides a seminal example of how informal rules underpin economic relations. He describes how the Maghribi, descendants of Jewish traders who immigrated to Tunisia, developed a distinct social identity within the larger Jewish population. Based on their shared social ties, language, and religion they formed an informal coalition, "an economic institution in which expectations, implicit contractual relations, and a specific information transmission mechanism supported the operation of a reputation mechanism" (1993: 525). This coalition enabled the Maghribi traders to expand around the Mediterranean during the eleventh century using overseas agents. Traders monitored their agents, shared information about agents' honesty, and collectively refused to hire agents accused of cheating by any Maghribi trader. The expectations generated by this information sharing and multilateral punishment mechanism deterred Maghribi traders from hiring non-member agents, and also deterred member agents from cheating or from seeking employment with non-Maghribis. This institution relied on a set of shared cultural rules of behavior that specified how to behave to be considered honest and to remain part of the traders' network. It functioned as an implicit contract between traders and agents (2006: 70).

1.1.4   Why do institutions exist?

Institutions arose to give "a guide to human interaction" and "reduce uncertainty by providing a structure to everyday life" (North, 1990a: 4). By making human behavior more predictable, both formal and informal institutions reduce the cost of transacting with others. As North puts it, because institutions permit impersonal transactions between strangers over time and at a distance even where neither self-enforcement by the parties to the transaction nor "trust" are viable ways to enforce rules (1987; 1990a: ch. 4), they are "the basic determinant of the performance of an economy" (2005: 48). Rules and norms that secure property rights, enforce contracts, promote public order, curb abuses of power, and the like also frame incentives that motivate people to "harness the potential of inclusive markets, encourage technological innovation, invest in people, and mobilize the talents and skills of a large number of individuals" (Acemoglu and Robinson, 2012: 79).

While informal rules are as old as human history, formal rules gained greater prominence later, in response to the growing complexity of societies, with increasing specialization and division of labor and the development of long-distance exchanges, aided by the development of writing and technological changes that lowered measurement costs (North, 1990a: ch. 6). As merchants began to seek higher returns by transacting with people outside their family, village, network, or guild, informal rules enforced by social ostracism would no longer suffice (as described by North and Thomas, 1973 [1999]; and Greif, 2006). Thus, governance of transactions through institutions enforced by third parties – such as property rights and contract laws enforced by courts – become crucial for reducing uncertainty (North, 1991) and lowering transaction costs (we describe this in more detail in Chapter 6).

1.1.5   Golden triangle

The NIE representation of institutions summarized above rests upon three key concepts: transaction costs, property rights, and contracts. These concepts form what has been termed the "golden triangle" of NIE, which we illustrate in Figure 1.1. The following three chapters define and discuss each of these concepts in detail; here we only briefly summarize their meaning and importance to NIE.

For NIE, a transaction is defined as the transfer of the rights to use a resource from one holder of rights to another, and *transaction costs* are the costs of establishing, transferring, and policing those rights (see Chapter 2). For example, even with face-to-face barter, the parties to the transaction must incur a cost in seeking a partner to the exchange, ascertaining the quality of the goods or services to be exchanged, and agreeing on a price (quantity). As this example suggests, at the micro-level, transaction costs depend on the attributes of the transaction at stake. But they also depend on the broader environment in which they are embedded. Thus, as Coase explained, transaction costs "depend on the institutions of a country: its legal system, its political system, its social system, its educational system, its culture, and so on" (1998: 72–3). Besides transaction costs, the NIE literature has been especially active in exploring how institutions affect *property rights*, understood as rights to use resources, which include both rights enforced by law, such as formal title to a house, and de facto rights, such as traditional ownership of a slum dwelling (Chapter 3). Another NIE cornerstone is *contracts*, defined as a mutual agreement between two or more parties determining the transfer and enforcement of rights. Contractual relationships structure a substantial part of economic activities (Chapter 4). For new institutionalists, understanding how institutions define and enforce property rights and how contracts structure and secure transactions as part of efforts to reduce transaction costs is fundamental to understanding how economies (and societies) function. At the micro-level, these concepts underpin the human choices about the ways they organize their activities (Chapter 5). At the macro-level, they shape the institutional environment of societies, including the nature of state and legal systems (Chapter 6). Transaction costs, property rights, and contracts are also key to the NIE perspective on how public policy is decided and implemented (Chapter 7) and our understanding of institutional change and development (Chapter 8).

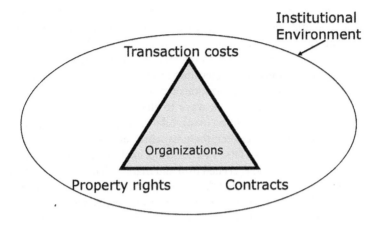

Figure 1.1   The golden triangle of NIE

1.2   The branches of NIE: Williamson, North, and Ostrom

1.2.1   Origins and founders

Where did these concepts originate? Ronald Coase initiated the movement that later led to new institutional economics[5] when he famously asked (1937), why are there firms; why are markets not sufficient to organize economic activities? He answered that using markets to organize transactions has a cost and there are conditions under which a firm can be less costly. Later (1960) Coase explicitly introduced the concept and broadened the role of transaction costs, showing that when transaction costs are positive – and they almost always are – institutions matter for the organization of economies. Coase's articles[6] inspired three scholars who played a central role in developing and diffusing NIE along its different branches: Williamson, North, and Ostrom.

---

[5]   The term "new institutional economics" was coined by Oliver Williamson (1975). He emphasized the organizational dimension of institutions and distinguished NIE from the old institutionalism. He credited Coase, Hayek, Arrow, Simon, and Chandler as the main sources of inspiration.

[6]   Coase writings are listed at: https://www.coase.org/coasepublications.htm.

At a time when mainstream economics was dominated by an almost exclusive focus on markets and price mechanisms, Oliver *Williamson* saw the potential of Coase's transaction cost approach as a way to analyze the variety of organizations (Williamson, 1975). He made the concept of transaction cost into an operational, micro-analytical tool by identifying the attributes that determine these costs and that explain the tradeoffs firms and other organizations face when their decision-makers must choose among alternative ways to develop economic activities (Williamson, 1971; 1975; 1985a; 1996). Like Coase, Williamson initially focused on the tradeoff between the polar cases of markets versus integrated firms (hierarchies), later extending his analysis to other arrangements that combined and exceeded firm and market characteristics (such as franchises), which he called "hybrids" (1996: ch.4). In the process, Williamson developed what is now transaction cost economics (TCE) and initiated a stream of research on contracts, which he introduced as a major means of monitoring the hazards that plague transactions, thereby reducing uncertainty (1971).

Parallel to Williamson's challenge to standard micro-economics, Douglass *North* became dissatisfied with the mainstream approach to growth and development with its focus on the accumulation of capital and the tradeoff between capital and labor. In his search for answers to Adam Smith's famous question: why are some countries rich and some countries poor? North increasingly saw institutions as the key explanation for growth and development (Davis and North, 1971; North and Thomas, 1973 [1999]; North, 1981; 1990a). He analyzed two variables as complementary determinants of the wealth of nations: property rights, as incentives to innovate, and transaction costs, as barriers to the expansion of trade.

Elinor *Ostrom* joined the movement later (1990; 1996; 2005). Ostrom focused on resources that are not privately or state owned but held by a community, such as common forests, shared fisheries, common irrigation systems, common lands, and the like. Her in-depth, empirical analysis of such common pool resources and their self-governance (1990) led her to focus on the institutions that support collective action and allow some communities to avoid the "tragedy of the commons," the overexploitation of resources held without state or private property rights. Like the other two Nobel laureates, she attracted a large following especially through the workshops she established with Vincent Ostrom at Indiana

University. Figure 1.2 introduces the NIE "family tree" including the names of some early followers, many of them past presidents or founding officers and members of the International Society for New Institutional Economics (ISNIE).[7]

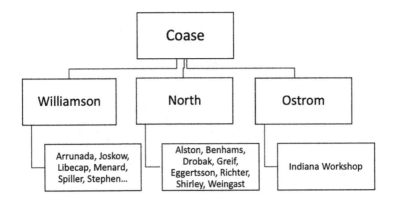

Figure 1.2   NIE family tree

NIE did not develop in a vacuum. There were other schools of thought and scholars who were not founders and, in some cases, not participants in NIE who nonetheless had an important influence, as we can see in Figure 1.3. These include Buchanan, Tulloch, and the field of public choice; Mancur Olson and his ideas about collective action; positive political scientists, such as Shepsle and Bates; and groundbreaking thinkers about property rights, such as Alchian, Barzel, Cheung, and Demsetz.

1.2.2   Multiple theories

As Figure 1.2 suggests, the NIE branches broadly correspond to the specific domains opened by Williamson, North, and Ostrom. Notwithstanding efforts to unite them into one big family (most notably through an international society),[8] the branches of the family tree are still growing

---

[7]   We are fully aware that there were numerous other early contributors and we apologize for those not mentioned.

[8]   Founded in 1997 in Saint-Louis, the International Society for New Institutional Economics (ISNIE) was later renamed the Society for Institutional and Organizational Economics (SIOE).

in different directions, although well attached to the central conceptual trunk. Even today, relatively few researchers attempt to combine these separate branches within a unified framework. NIE may be best portrayed as a movement towards a synthesis that has not yet arrived.

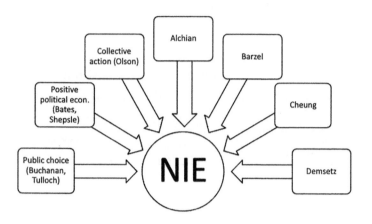

Figure 1.3   Influences on NIE's early development

Nevertheless, there is a fundamental agreement among NIE researchers about: (1) behavioral assumptions; (2) fundamental concepts of the "golden triangle"; and (3) key elements of a multidimensional research agenda. Aggregating across its branches, NIE emerges as a configuration distinct from alternative approaches.

1.3   NIE's assumptions and methods

1.3.1   Behavioral assumptions

Most contributors to NIE assume *bounded rationality*, that human behavior is "intendedly rational, but only limitedly so" (Simon, 1947 [1961]:

xxiv).[9] "Limits on man's ability to comprehend and compute in the face of complexity and uncertainty" constrain economic actors who try to make intractable choices tractable by "looking for satisfactory choices instead of optimal ones," "replacing abstract global goals with tangible sub goals," and "dividing the decision making task among many specialists" (Simon, 1979: 494 sq.). While endorsing Simon's view, NIE goes beyond those economists who assume that the source of bounded rationality is purely an information processing problem. In NIE, individuals not only face information constraints and cognitive limitations, their choices are also shaped by belief systems and societal norms (North, 2005; Ostrom, 2005; 2014; Greif, 2006). Moreover, although individuals matter, for many NIE scholars interactions among rational individuals cannot fully explain the emergence, characteristics, and dynamics of institutional settings. These new institutionalists presume that the collective action in which institutions are rooted exceeds the sum of the parts.

Opportunism is another important NIE behavioral assumption.[10] The idea that agents' choices are motivated by self-interest is deeply rooted in economics, going back to the famous *Fable of the Bees* (Mandeville, 1732 [1988]) or the Smithian conception of the "invisible hand."[11] However, NIE takes opportunism in a different direction, treating it as "self-interest seeking with guile, which includes calculated efforts to mislead, obfuscate, and otherwise confuse" partner(s) to a transaction (Williamson, 1985a: 51). This form of opportunism refers to the strategic behavior of agents taking advantage of the uncertainty surrounding transactions and the bounded rationality of the other party(ies) to distort agreements to

---

[9]   Neoclassical and game theoretic models presume rational individuals are motivated to maximize their utility, possess extensive information on both the available alternatives and their outcomes, and have a clear ranking of their preferences.

[10] Opportunism was initially emphasized by Williamson (1985a: 47 sq.; 1996: 47–8, 378).

[11] Opportunism is at the core of agency theory, which assumes that agents (e.g., the managers of a firm) will act in their own self-interest in ways that principals (e.g., the owners of a firm) cannot monitor because of information asymmetries. This shared focus on incentives may explain why some authors consider agency theory to be a part of NIE (Furubotn and Richter, 1997: 22–3). However, the two differ in focus. In brief, agency theory focuses on the design of an optimal contract to motivate a rational agent to behave according to the preferences of the principal. NIE emphasizes both *ex ante* and *ex post* manipulation of agreements between partners to a transaction.

their advantage, *ex ante* in the negotiation phase but mainly *ex post* at the time of enforcement.[12] North (1984; 1990a) also analyzed how the risk of opportunism hindered the development of impersonal exchange. Opportunism raises an important question in NIE: how to make commitment to bargains credible? Credibility can be achieved either through institutional guarantees (such as laws securing property rights or reducing regulatory discretion) and/or complex contractual agreements that increase transaction costs, thus reducing the benefits of exchange (Levy and Spiller, 1994; Spiller, 2009).

NIE's assumptions of bounded rationality and opportunism differ from neoclassical models, and introduce behavioral factors shaping the collective action that is crucial to the establishment and enforcement of the rules of the game characterizing modern social orders (North, Wallis and Weingast, 2009; Acemoglu and Robinson, 2019). This approach also connects NIE to sociology (e.g., Powell and DiMaggio, 1991; Brinton and Nee, 1998), political science (e.g., Olson, 1965; McCubbins, Noll and Weingast, 1987; 1989; Weingast, 1989; 2005), and legal studies (e.g., Hadfield, 2005; Bernstein, 2019), notwithstanding their differences in goals and methodologies.

1.3.2   Economic assumptions

NIE is distinguished from neoclassical models (and much of other disciplines such as political science or law) in its strong prior assumption that unknown or understudied institutional details lie at the heart of socio-economic puzzles. New institutionalists' first instinct is to ask: do distortions in formal rules or informal norms and their enforcement explain the phenomenon in question?

---

[12]   According to Williamson (1985a: 47 sq.), the concept of opportunism differs from the distinction (borrowed from the insurance literature) between adverse selection and moral hazard. Opportunism does not necessarily originate from informational problems and does not presume rational behavior. It does not consider agents as systematically opportunist, but views them as calculative enough to anticipate possible hazards posed to transactions and to look for safeguards within the agreement or through external enforcers (e.g., laws protecting property rights) (Williamson, 1996: ch.10).

As the rest of this book shows, although NIE scholars acknowledge neo-classical theory's positive contribution to our understanding of the price mechanism, NIE's assumptions diverge significantly from the neoclassical. NIE replaces the costless, frictionless *market* of neoclassical models with one in which transactions have costs determined by the institutional environment and the nature of the transaction. NIE changes the perfect *property rights* of neoclassical models into rights that are often poorly defined or poorly enforced. NIE opens the neoclassical black box of the *firm* and explores choices between firms, markets, and other organizational modalities emphasizing positive transaction costs and contracts that are incomplete and plagued by hazards. Neoclassical models usually assume an informed, objective, and efficient legal system, while NIE emphasizes the role of private ordering to avoid costly, arbitrary, and uncertain legal systems. The neoclassical *state* is often portrayed as an objective regulator aiming to maximize social welfare. NIE accepts the public choice view that the motivations of individual state actors are important (Buchanan and Tullock, 1962), and is concerned with the way constitutional institutions (such as dictatorship versus democracy or parliamentary versus presidential systems) and behavioral norms (such as civic activism) frame the incentives for legal, political, and bureaucratic actors. Also central to NIE are collective actions by citizens and their effects on public policy. Finally, NIE rejects the neoclassical thesis that *growth* is primarily determined by capital stock in the short run and technological change in the long run, in favor of the premise that institutions are crucial for determining growth.

1.3.3   Methodology

NIE is defined not only by its assumptions, but also by its drive to analyze empirically the "big" questions of economic organization and development. This, even as neoclassical models have been excluding questions and assuming away frictions and institutions to meet the requirements of more and more sophisticated mathematical tools, with methodological rectitude prevailing over content. Instead NIE scholars have prioritized content, working to adapt analytical tools and expand data to allow causal identification without ignoring institutions' multifaceted and multidimensional characteristics (Skarbek, 2020). New institutionalists freely exploit the tools of econometrics, but also make extensive use of lab and field experiments and case studies. They have initiated efforts to combine qualitative and quantitative methods more rigorously, from Douglass

North's development with Robert Fogel of cliometrics (the application of economic theory and statistical tools to history), Ostrom's extensive case studies of common pool institutions, analytic narratives applying formal modeling and rational choice theory to derive empirically tested hypotheses from particular cases (Bates et al., 1998), and recently Skarbek's (2020) proposal to derive causal identification from qualitative data through comparative case studies and process tracing.[13]

1.4 NIE's relation to game theory and old institutional economics

1.4.1   A complex relation to game theory

New institutionalists generally have adopted the "institutions as rules-of-the game" perspective that we follow in this book. But game theory's "institutions as the equilibrium outcome of a game" has also been influential among some leading figures of the NIE movement (e.g., Milgrom, North and Weingast, 1989; Ostrom, 1990; 2005; Greif, 1993; 2006; Crawford and Ostrom, 1995).

Simply put, game theory views an institution as "a regularity in social behavior that is agreed to by all members of society, specifies behavior in specific recurrent situations, and is either self-policed or policed by some external authority" (Schotter, 1981: 11). Such regularities emerge from mutually understood preferences and the optimizing behavior of actors (Crawford and Ostrom, 1995: 582; also Aoki, 2001: 4 sq.). This approach assumes that rational agents are making individual choices based on extensive information and shared knowledge about the state of the world and the "rules of the game." However, North asserts that game theory "does not provide us with a theory of the underlying costs of transacting and how these costs are altered by different institutional structures" (1990a: 15). Moreover, in a game, rules are assumed to be defined *ex ante*,

---

[13]   Process tracing methodically traces causality from changes in independent variables through intervening variables to changes in the dependent variable (Skarbek, 2020).

whereas NIE is preoccupied with the explanation for institutions' rise and change.[14]

1.4.2   How does NIE differ from old (original) institutionalism?

A recurrent question is how NIE relates to what Coase and others have termed the "old institutional economics" (OIE). Coase (1984) discarded OIE as a-theoretical[15] (also Rutherford, 1994: ch. 7; 2001; Williamson, 2010), a position obviously challenged by authors closer to OIE (e.g., Hodgson, 1989; 2015: ch. 1; Groenewegen, Spithoven and van den Berg, 2010: ch. 2). Retrospectively and away from the polemic, we can summarize the connections and divergences between NIE and OIE.

Perhaps the most pervasive unity between OIE and NIE is in their common theme "that institutions matter a great deal, and that economists need to think hard about the ways in which institutions shape economic behavior and outcomes, and are themselves shaped by economic, political, and ideological factors" (Rutherford, 2001: 190). However, while agreeing that institutions matter, NIE differs from OIE in how its adherents approach their subject. Probably one of the most important distinctions was NIE's approach to neoclassical theory. OIE rejected neoclassical's fundamental assumptions including the understanding of markets as an "invisible hand" operating through supply and demand (Rutherford, 2001: 175), while NIE acknowledges the role of the "invisible hand," although under very restrictive circumstances. In the tradition of Veblen, Commons, and other American institutionalists, Hodgson (1998) views the radical rejection of rationality as one of OIE's most important assumptions, motivating its rejection of neoclassical models. NIE proposes a more nuanced approach to rationality. Most NIE contributors acknowledge that in highly competitive markets for standardized goods – circumstances that are closest to the zero transaction cost world – economic actors who behave like the rational *homo oeconomicus* of neoclassical models will be more likely to survive. However, NIE considers this situation exceptional.

---

[14]   Typically, in experimental economics, which has been largely inspired by game theory, the institutional setting is defined before the actual experiment begins.

[15]   "Without a theory they had nothing to pass on except a mass of descriptive material waiting for a theory, or a fire" Coase (1984: 230). Earlier Koopmans (1947) referred to OIE as "measurement without theory."

In most situations, economic agents may be "calculative" (Williamson, 1996: ch. 10), but they operate in highly imperfect markets within the constraints of their strictly bounded rationality (Simon, 1957; 1979), and as a result the outcome is plagued by uncertainties and differs from the one predicted by neoclassical models. North verged nearer to OIE when he argued that subjective perceptions of reality (what he termed "mental models") played a major part in human choices (2005). Nevertheless, although North's work on mental models, norms, and ideology resembles OIE, it maintains calculative actors in, for example, the importance of incentives to innovation. In North's view, incentives are precisely why institutions such as well-defined property rights matter so much.

Additionally, new institutionalists readily employ theoretical and analytical tools of neoclassical economics, distinguishing their analyses from the descriptive approach that prevailed in OIE. Indeed, the main gap between NIE and OIE likely comes from NIE's coherent and tightly interdependent set of concepts, summarized in the golden triangle, that foster empirical testing and feed a particularly rich research agenda (Menard and Shirley, 2018). As Williamson asserted, "whereas the price theoretic approach to economics would become the 'dominant paradigm' during the twentieth century (Melvin W. Reder, 1999: 43), [old] institutional economics was mainly relegated to the history of thought because it failed to advance a positive research agenda that was replete with predictions and empirical testing (Stigler as reported in Edmund W. Kitch, 1983: 170). Stalwarts notwithstanding, old institutional economics 'ran itself into the sand.'" (Williamson, 2010: 674)

1.5   Conclusion

NIE offers an alternative paradigm that has motivated substantial changes in research in economics and other social sciences and opened exciting new research agendas (Menard and Shirley, 2018). The next chapters summarize essential contributions and suggest open research questions. However, the reader must remain aware that the resulting impression of a single, monolithic theory is wrong. NIE retains its open, dynamic arborescence. What makes this movement coherent is the set of fundamental concepts that provides a framework underlying and partially unifying the diversity of analyses and perspectives, and we turn to them next.

PART I

Fundamental concepts

2 Transaction costs

To new institutional economics (NIE) contributors, transactions are the basic unit of analysis in economics (Williamson, 1985a: 18). Why so? Because they view economics as primarily concerned with the transfers of rights to use goods and services for production and exchange, transfers that are central for benefitting from the division of labor and specialization (Coase, 1998). In that respect, the NIE approach differs profoundly from the neoclassical perspective: NIE looks at economics through the lens of the transfer of rights to use a resource; the neoclassical paradigm looks at economics through the lens of trade in goods and services on markets.

The NIE approach has substantial consequences. At the micro-level, it means focusing on how economic activities are actually organized in response to transaction costs. At the macro-level, it means focusing on how institutional and organizational structures affect performance, development, and growth. This chapter briefly presents the central concepts of transaction and transaction costs (2.1), the origin and misinterpretations of the "Coase theorem" (2.2), and the implementation as well as the extension of the transaction costs approach (2.3). Examples of the application of transaction costs analysis at the micro- and macro-level are developed in Parts II and III of this book.

2.1   Core concepts: from transactions to transaction costs

The concept of transaction is tightly intertwined with the idea that organizing transactions involves costs. We introduce first the NIE definition of transaction and then that of transaction costs, and follow with some important consequences of this transactional approach.

2.1.1   Transactions

Transactions broadly defined are the transfer of rights to use a resource. All transactions involve at least two parties, which explains why a substantial part of the literature on transactions has focused on bargaining and contracts (see Chapter 4). When I rent a car to go out of town for the weekend, I acquire from the owner of the car (the rental company, which might well be the subsidiary of another company) the right to use this car under certain conditions. For example, I must commit to assume certain liabilities and to return the car in an appropriate condition as specified in the rental contract.

This example shows how the concept of transaction overlaps with that of property rights, with these rights defined as "the rights of individuals to the use of resources" (Alchian, 1965: 817; more on this concept in Chapter 3). The right to use is seldom limitless; it is usually constrained by restrictions specified in a transactional agreement or imposed by external rules. For example, a requirement to get the rented car insured might be imposed by the rental car company or made compulsory by the law. In that respect, transactions usually allow only limited use of a good or service since they are deeply embedded in institutions delineating the domain of acceptable usage. In the car rental example, the contract is embedded in contract law and my usage of the car is constrained by traffic regulation. It also means that economic rights are intertwined with legal rights (Cheung, 1969b). Insurance might be compulsory, but its coverage may vary, which translates into variations in cost.

Besides institutional embeddedness, for a transaction to happen the good or service to be traded must be technologically separable from other goods and services. This requirement explains why a transaction is frequently described as occurring "when a good or service is transferred across a technologically separable interface" (Williamson, 1985a: 1). For example, melting iron is a continuous process that cannot be segmented, while transportation of iron slates can be separated from the melting operation. This seems a simple idea but it has important implications. As soon as separability is technologically possible, the question becomes how to organize the process at stake. The economics of organization then emerge as a core component of the transactional approach (see Chapter 5) and technological considerations are integral to that approach. Indeed, technology and organization are tightly intertwined, with technology constantly changing what is tradeable and how. For example, technological developments have increasingly allowed unbundling the parts of a cell phone so that they can be produced and assembled in places around the world, while it has also bundled previously separate functions so that the purchase of a cell phone now buys a camera, a calculator, a calendar, and so on.

Hence, for a transaction to exist requires (1) the transfer of rights among parties, (2) the usage of these rights under constraints that might be specified within the transactional agreement and/or by external rules, and (3) goods or services that are technologically separable. Thus understood, transactions are not limited to transfers of rights on markets; non-market transactions are continuously conducted within firms as well as among a variety of other organizational arrangements, such as public bureaus, franchising, strategic alliances, cooperatives, and the like.

2.1.2   Transaction costs

Every transaction is exposed to "transactional failures" (Williamson, 1971). To be consummated, a transaction requires technological and institutional supports that entail costs. On the technological side, from the Code of Hammurabi engraved in stone to modern contracts, parties to a transaction need the means to communicate. This is true even for an agreement based on a handshake, since even that requires the use of language, which entails the cost of learning a common language. On the institutional side, the transfer of rights may occur through different organizational arrangements, with markets being only one solution among a set of alternatives (see Chapter 5). Whatever the arrangement chosen, any transfer of rights incurs the cost of delineating and policing those rights, a necessary condition for transacting parties to commit.

Once the existence of transaction costs is acknowledged, the next question is: what are the causes and sources of transaction costs? Coase pioneered the investigation of that question in two highly influential articles. In "The nature of the firm" (1937), he raised what became a central issue in economics: if markets are efficient, why are there firms? His answer emphasizes the comparative costs of using the price mechanism versus the costs of organizing transactions through management. In the "Problem of social cost" (1960), Coase pointed out the key components of market transactions, stating that: "In order to carry out a market transaction it is necessary to discover who it is that one wishes to deal with, to inform people that one wishes to deal and on what terms, to conduct negotiations leading up to a bargain, to draw up the contract, to undertake the inspection needed to make sure that the terms of the contract are being observed, and so on" (1960: 15). Dahlman (1979: 148) translated these requirements into an often quoted statement identifying transaction costs as the combination of "search and information costs, bargaining and decision costs, policing and enforcement costs" involved in the organization of market exchange.

These specifications tend to overemphasize the organization of transactions in the context of market exchanges, in which transaction costs are "the cost of using the price mechanism" (Coase, 1937). Beyond Coase's initial insight, much less has been said about transactions carried out within the firm. What about the "managerial" or "administrative" costs involved in setting up, maintaining, and operating resources and their transfer across technologically separable interfaces within the firm (Furubotn and Richter, 1997: 44 sq.) or, for that matter, within alternative organizational solutions, for example within strategic alliances? Coase already provides some guidance, pointing out the need to comparatively assess the costs of transfers through markets versus in-house, stating that "a firm will tend to expand until the costs of organizing an extra transaction within the firm become equal to the costs of carrying out the same transaction by means of an exchange on the open market or the costs of organizing in another firm" (Coase, 1937: 395). Cheung (1969b), a disciple of Coase, went a step further in showing the relevance of the transactional approach to understand the variety of modalities through which parties can organize transactions, thus facing complex tradeoffs. Using Chinese data on sharecropping, he pointed out "the presence of a variety of contractual arrangements under the *same* constraint of competition" and the role of transaction costs in opting for a specific arrangement.[1]

The idea that transaction costs encompass far more than the costs of market exchanges led scholars to reconsider and extend the concept of transaction costs to capture the diversity of arrangements through which transactions can be organized. Based on a more encompassing definition of transaction costs, Allen (1991: 3; 2000) contrasted the narrow approach

---

[1]   In the same article, Cheung argues that transaction costs differ because physical attributes, institutional factors, and modalities of negotiation and enforcement differ.

favored by neoclassical economics, which identifies transactions and their costs solely as the trading of goods and services through markets, thus identifying them as equivalent to taxes, with the new institutionalist approach, which considers transactions costs as the resources used to establish, transfer, and maintain property rights (see Box 2.1). Further, transaction costs vary according to the choice of organizational modalities (or "governance structure"[2]) chosen to carry out the transaction as well as with the institutional conditions framing these rights and their transfer (see also Alston et al., 2018: 68).[3]

Box 2.1   Neoclassical vs NIE approach to transaction costs: Robinson Crusoe and Friday

In an article that helped clarify the concept of transaction costs, Allen (2000; 895 sq.) criticized neoclassical economics (e.g., Niehans, 1987) for its narrow definition of transaction costs as the result of frictions in trading activities, frictions typically caused by information asymmetries, transportation costs, taxes. With this definition, transactions costs can be introduced into a standard equilibrium model to reach a first best solution.

However, as Allen pointed out, defining transaction costs as information or transportation costs is inadequate. Consider Robinson Crusoe, shipwrecked on his island, alone before the arrival of Friday. He faced information and transportation costs, even though there was no transacting going on!

In the broader concept prevailing in the new institutional approach, transaction costs encompass the multidimensional components that contribute to the establishment, allocation, and monitoring of rights to use a resource. For example, Cheung (1989: 77) defines transaction costs as "a spectrum of institutional costs including those of information, of negotiation, of drawing up and enforcing contracts, of delineating and policing property rights, of monitoring performance, and

---

[2]   Williamson defines "governance structure" as "the institutional matrix within which transactions are negotiated and executed" (1979: 239; also 1996: 378).

[3]   Medema (2020: 1068 sq.) provides extensive indications on the different approaches to transaction costs.

of changing institutional arrangements." These costs do not exist in the solitary world of Robinson Crusoe. They emerge with the arrival of Friday, when arrangements must be made to organize the use of the scarce resources available. We enter into a world of alternative organizational solutions, each of which has different costs that must be assessed comparatively. Welcome to the world of second-best![4]

2.1.3   Consequences

One of the profound consequences of the property rights interpretation of transaction costs is that it reinforces that there are alternative ways to allocate these rights and to organize their transactions so that decision-makers face tradeoffs. Although it mainly focuses on the costs of market transactions and the role of the definition and allocation of property rights in overcoming externalities, "The problem of social costs" (Coase, 1960) already emphasized the need to consider and compare alternative solutions to the allocation of rights.[5] However, Coase's contribution was largely intuitive. A full-fledged theory of transaction costs was still needed to illuminate the transactional logic behind the tradeoff among different organizational solutions and the role played by institutions in shaping the organization and achievement of transactions.

This unfinished business attracted the attention of Williamson. Dissatisfied with existing theories of vertical integration which he confronted while working at the US Department of Justice and which mostly assumed that businesses merge in order to dominate markets through monopoly power,[6] he turned to Coasian transaction costs as an explanation.[7] A crucial point made by Coase (1937: 389) was that "It is surely important to enquire why coordination is the work of the price mech-

---

[4]   As well summarized by Medema (2020: 1051): "in the real world of positive transaction costs, all coordination mechanisms – markets, firms, and government – are costly and imperfect, meaning that there is no route to the optimum."

[5]   In his conclusion, Coase stated: "Furthermore we have to take into account the costs involved in operating the various social arrangements (whether it be the working of a market or of a government department), as well as the costs involved in moving to a new system" (1960: 44).

[6]   Coase (1972 [1988]) made a similar point.

[7]   Although Williamson paid tribute to Commons for having introduced the idea "that the transaction is the ultimate unit of microeconomic analysis"

anisms in one case and of the entrepreneur in another ..." Williamson (1975) adopted a micro-analytical approach to explain this tradeoff, which he reformulated as the choice between acquiring a needed good or service through markets (to "buy") or producing it within the organization (to "make"). He showed that understanding this "make-or-buy" tradeoff requires considering the "attributes" of the transaction at stake. The logic is straightforward: when competition pushes transactors to minimize costs, they must consider the characteristics of the transaction at stake (its attributes in Williamson's terminology) if they are to adopt the least costly organizational solution. The Williamsonian model (1975; 1985a), which has inspired thousands of empirical tests, focuses on three attributes, understood as "the principal dimensions with respect to which transactions differ" (Williamson, 1985b: 181): (1) the uncertainty surrounding a transaction (a point already made by Coase in 1937), (2) the specificity of the assets needed to make the transaction possible, and (3) the frequency with which the transaction happens. Our car rental example illustrates.

Uncertainty, leading to "unprogrammed adaptations" (Williamson, 1971: 113) may come from moral hazard (the misbehavior of the driver due to improper insurance or rental contracts) or adverse selection (the driver has been poorly trained). Specific investments by the car rental company include a fleet of cars and offices outposts for different parts of its service territory. And the frequency of rental agreements impacts the cost of monitoring these agreements. Chapter 5 provides more detail on the explosion of research on the theory of organization that followed this breakthrough, often identified as transaction cost economics (TCE), which led to the award of the Nobel Prize to Williamson in 2009.

2.2   The "Coase theorem": origin and misinterpretations

This prominent role of transactions and their costs did not percolate easily through economics. Paradoxically, and to the dismay of Coase and his followers, the initial and long predominant neoclassical interpreta-

---

(1975: ix), his conception of transaction and transaction costs is definitely Coasian (see Chapter 1).

tion of Coase's concept of transaction costs was stuck in what became the infamous "Coase theorem" and its radical assumption about "the strange world of costless transactions" (Furubotn and Richter, 1997: 8). Notwithstanding Coase's own view and the general agreement in NIE and beyond that transaction costs exist, are positive, and differ from production costs, a resilient view that focuses on the so-called 'Coase Theorem' and remains the source of disconcerting interpretations even today.[8]

Box 2.2   The origins of the "Coase theorem"

The Coase theorem, which enjoys such renown in economics, got its start over cocktails.

In 1959, Ronald Coase, then a professor at the University of Virginia, had just written "The Federal Communications Commission" (1959). In it, he argued controversially that the FCC should auction radio spectrum instead of assigning it by fiat, asserting that assignment by fiat raised the ugly possibility of political control over freedom of the press. Auctions would end that specter and allow private investors to trade their rights in order to maximize investment and productivity.

Coase contended that if rights were well defined and freely tradeable on perfectly competitive markets, it would not matter what the initial assignment of rights were, they would be negotiated and traded in ways that maximize the value of their usage. To a group of economists at the University of Chicago, this argument seemed like "heresy," so they invited Coase to Chicago to defend it. The subsequent discussion over drinks at the home of Aaron Director, then editor of the Journal of Law and Economics, included such luminaries as Milton Friedman, Arnold Harberger, and George Stigler. Stigler later described the meeting in his autobiography as an "eureka moment" (1988).

According to Stigler, at the beginning of the discussion, the assembled economists voted 20 to 1 against Coase; (Coase cast the only vote in his

---

[8]   For an extensive review and discussion of the literature on the Coase theorem, see Medema (2020). Medema also shows (in section 6) how the "Coase theorem" and its zero transaction costs assumption permeated almost all domains of economics and influenced numerous contributions in legal studies, political science, etc.

favor). After much discussion, Coase prevailed and all 21 voted in his favor and asked him to write up his argument for the Journal of Law and Economics. That article became "The problem of social cost," one of the most cited articles in economics and law. Stigler coined the term "Coase theorem," which he described succinctly: "under perfect competition, private and social costs will be equal ..." (1966: 113).

What Stigler's snapshot of the "Coase theorem" in Box 2.2 means is that "in the absence of transaction costs, the allocation of resources is independent of the distribution of property rights" (Allen, 2000: 897). Indeed, what Coase showed in "The problem of social cost" is that under the standard assumptions of economic theory – perfect competition, perfect information, frictionless bargaining, in other words, a world of zero transaction costs – rational actors can negotiate a bargain that allocates rights in a way that will maximize production, regardless of the initial assignment of those rights (Shirley, 2013: 244; Medema, 2020: 1072 sq.). In a world of costless transactions, as long as property rights are fully specified,[9] efficient outcomes will arise through transacting regardless of which party initially owns which right and which institutions organize transactions. The "Coase theorem" thus assumes that an efficient outcome can be reached without consideration for the way property rights are allocated and transferred.

Coase's 1960 article unambiguously argued that this standard economic assumption of zero transaction costs is unrealistic. As Coase later explained, "The world of zero transaction costs has often been described as a Coasian world. Nothing could be further from the truth. It is the world of modern economic theory, one which I was hoping to persuade economists to leave" (Coase, 1988b: 174). "The problem of social cost" and several other contributions by Coase were "contrasting a frictionless world with the real world of costly coordination" (Medema, 2020: 1061).

The distinction between a world of zero transaction costs and one with positive transaction costs is therefore fundamental, and key to understanding the opposition of NIE contributors to the standard neoclassical

---

[9]   Medema (2020: 1072) emphasizes the importance of two other underlying assumptions to the "theorem": utilities are transferable and information is costless.

interpretation. In an article written for the Nobel Committee when it was considering awarding Coase the prize, Barzel and Kochin rightly asserted that "Coase's explicit separation of the zero and positive transaction cost models made economists aware of the need to spell out the transaction cost assumptions under which analysis is conducted ... [G]iven that transaction is costly, whether it is carried out in the market or by government, Coase pointed out the need to compare outcomes of actions carried out under different institutional settings" (1992: 22).

Understanding Coase's argument and assessing its multiple consequences for our understanding of the variety of organizational arrangements and the role of institutions in framing our economies should be part of the core of economists' agendas. One might expect that economists reading "The problem of social cost" would have learned this lesson and rethink their assumption that institutions and transaction costs can be omitted from their models. Unfortunately, that did not happen. To the contrary, most economists incorrectly assumed that Coase believed that transaction costs were usually zero.[10] But for some few scholars, Coase's argument lit an intellectual fire that blazed into the new institutional economics in the mid-1970s.

2.3   Implementation and extension of the transaction cost approach

Ronald Coase was right when he stated (1972 [1988]: 63) that "The nature of the firm" was "an article much cited and little used" (1972 [1988]: 63). Yet, surprisingly it is this article, which focused on the reason why firms exist without an explicit reference to transaction costs, more than "The problem of social cost" which explicitly introduced transaction costs[11]

---

[10]   According to Shirley (2013), "A survey of 45 textbooks found that 80% of them misrepresented Coase's arguments (Butler and Garnett, 2003). Another, later survey of 40 of the most cited and most recent articles on the Coase Theorem concluded that 75% of them misrepresented Coase's viewpoint (Yalcintas 2010)."

[11]   As noted by Williamson (1975: 3), Commons already introduced the idea of transaction as "the ultimate unit of economic investigation" (Commons, 1934: 4–8).

that initially caught the attention of economists.[12] However, two leading figures changed this situation, giving an impulse to research built on the concept of transaction cost and initiating NIE as a powerful movement among economists and beyond.

We already mentioned the role of Oliver Williamson in that respect (see 2.1 above). Besides establishing transaction costs as critical to understanding industrial organization (1975; 1985a), he pointed out the role of this concept as central to a "comparative institutional approach to the study of economic organization" (1985a: 387), opening a rich stream of research that we detail in Chapter 5. Douglass North, the other leading figure at the origin of NIE, established transaction costs as a tool to understanding the economic role of institutions, as well as development and growth (North and Thomas 1973 [1999]; North 1981; 1990a), launching a new domain of research explored in Chapters 6 to 8. Williamson and North thus initiated a movement that describes the major impact that transactions and their associated costs have on our understanding of how human activities are organized and the role of institutions as a major determinant framing these costs. Subsequently, the concept has been extended to analyze numerous institutional dimensions. For example, Arrow early on defined transaction costs as "the cost of running the economic system" (1969: 48). More recently and in the same vein, Allen (2012: 19) described transaction costs as "those costs necessary to establish and maintain any system of rules and rights."

These extensions capture the idea that transactions are deeply embedded in institutions, making transaction costs an integral part of the institutional setting. One outcome of this broader point of view is the introduction of the concept of "political transaction costs" as distinct from economic transaction costs (see North, 1990b; also Dixit, 1996; Furubotn and Richter, 1997: 43 sq., Caballero and Arias, 2013; Caballero and Soto-Oñate, 2016). While economic transactions are trades in the right to use a resource, political transactions transfer the temporary right to exercise political authority (Moe, 1990; Caballero and Soto-Oñate, 2016). Economic transaction costs are the costs of organizing pro-

---

[12]   Medema (2020, section 4) extensively reviewed the highly critical reactions among leading economists to the concept of transaction costs following the publication of "The problem of social cost." Fisher (1977) synthesized this opposition qualifying the concept as "tautological."

duction and exchange through different organizational arrangements, for example organizing distribution through franchising rather than through company-owned outlets. Political transaction costs "arise from the specific political institutions underlying political exchange in different polities" (North, 1990b: 364). Just as economic transaction costs rise with uncertainty, political transactions costs are the costs of striking unstable bargains under conditions of high uncertainty, where actors and interests are often obscure, there is no third-party enforcement, agreements are tacit and incomplete contracts, and outcomes can be abruptly overturned by the next election (Caballero and Arias, 2013; Caballero and Soto-Oñate, 2016). Political actors try to devise structures that aim to reduce these transaction costs and allow durable and enforceable bargains (for more details, see Chapter 7). Weingast and Marshall (1988) provides an example of this (Box 2.3).

Box 2.3   Political transaction costs

The concept of transaction cost has reached audiences far beyond economics, bridging the gap between different disciplines, particularly political science, where numerous contributions analyze the high transaction cost of reaching stable coalitions in highly imperfect political markets.

In a pioneering article, Weingast and Marshall (1988) examined the functioning of the US Congress through the lens of what they called "the new economics of organization." In this framing, public policies are the result of a series of bargains among various interests represented by legislators seeking reelection. Like economic transactions, political bargains have high transactions costs arising from imperfect information, opportunism, and the instability of political markets.

Weingast and Marshall assumed that congressmen represent heterogeneous groups of interests located within their districts, that political parties have limited capacities to constrain legislators, and that bills require a majority to be adopted. However, they differed from the prevailing view that legislators trade votes (or logrolling). The problem with treating legislative exchange of votes as similar to market exchange is that most "political" trades are not simultaneous. Today's legislation depends on future legislative events and expected benefits from legislation occurring in the future, raising problems of observability and the possibility that parties renege on agreements when circumstances change (ex post opportunism).

To circumvent the threat to durability and enforceability of bargains created by these political hazards, US legislators constructed alternative institutional solutions to vote trading. A key component was the committee system, which embedded the rights to control specific items of the political agenda. Operating under specific conditions (e.g., individual assignment to a limited number of seats, seniority system, bidding mechanism to assign vacant seats), this system facilitated enforcement of bargains. For example, members from farmers' districts sitting on agriculture committees and seeking farm benefits had to take into account and bargain with members of other committees, for instance members from urban districts sitting on welfare committees providing subsidies for food for the poor. In this institutional arrangement, sticking to the agreement so as to secure future bargains was a strong incentive to credibly commit.

Weingast and Marshall (1988) concluded that the institutional rules framing the action of these committees mitigated the "contractual problems" and allowed durable political coalitions.

The concept of political transaction costs is "built on the assumptions of costly information, of subjective models on the part of the actors to explain their environment and of imperfect enforcement of agreements" (North, 1990b: 355), allowing new institutionalists to escape the "a-institutional world of neoclassical theory." It thus complements the economic concept of transaction costs, opening the way to a more relevant analysis of those areas in which the two types of cost overlap. Recent illustrations can be found in Barzel (2000), North, Wallis and Weingast (2009), North et al. (2013), and Alston et al. (2018). Other important developments in NIE analysis of public policies and the nature and role of the state are discussed in Chapters 6 to 8.

2.4   Conclusions

The idea that transactions provide the basic unit of economic analysis is at the core of NIE. To new institutionalists, the economy is primarily about the transfer of usage rights, with the actual production and exchange of goods and services resulting from the nature and characteristics of these rights and the conditions of their transfer. Another key contribution is the demonstration that, whatever the type of rights at stake, there are different ways to organize these transfers, which entail different costs, called transaction costs. Identifying transaction costs and assessing their role in competing institutional arrangements provide the foundation to the modern economics of organization and institutions.

These ideas have stimulated a huge outpouring of research, yet there are still exciting opportunities for future study, particularly the need to better assess the comparative costs of integration versus alternative arrangements, to better identify and characterize the specific internal properties of various institutional settings and to embed these developments in more formalized models (Gibbons, 2010).

The concept of transaction costs has relevance far beyond the domain of economics. The contributions of the three founders of NIE, Coase, North, and Williamson, later joined by Elinor Ostrom (1990; 2005) have progressively influenced many other disciplines, from management to sociology, law, political science, and many others (Macher and Richman, 2008; Menard and Shirley, 2018; Medema, 2020). Indeed, transferring rights involves many different dimensions and might occur in many different contexts, such as political systems, public bureaucracies, and so on, which requires adaptation of the concepts to these different settings. Much of the earlier research on these issues has focused on mature democracies, but there is need for more analysis of non- and weak democracies.

There is important value-added in NIE's transactional approach. It has already thrown new light on the organization of economic activities at the micro-level and enlightened our understanding of the key role of institutions in shaping transaction costs and the role of transaction costs in shaping the way institutions work. It also has important implications for policy. Since the organization and costs of transactions matter, finding the appropriate match between institutional arrangements and the way rights are allocated revolutionizes the meaning of efficiency. As pointed out by Coase (1991 [2005]), in a world of positive transaction costs assigning rights to those who can use them most productively and reducing the institutional costs of transferring these rights are central to performance and, ultimately, growth and development.

However, we must be cautious when using the concepts of transaction and transaction costs to explore new territories that we not transform them into "catch-all" concepts providing nothing more than *ex post* rationalization. The coming chapters substantiate the ideas introduced above, with appropriate cautions.

3 Property rights

Property rights are among the most critical institutions in any society. Depending on how they are defined and enforced, they affect the scope for markets, firms, and other productive organizations; the extent of investment and innovation; and the losses from environmental degradation. Indeed, a crucial reason why institutions matter for economic performance is that they delineate and enforce property rights.

NIE's definition of property rights is dynamic and goes well beyond the legal definition (3.1). Private property rights are deeply intertwined with NIE's core concepts of transactions, incentives, and contracts, and are the focus of much of this chapter (3.2). The rise of impersonal institutions to define and defend private property rights is also a central issue, helping explain the rise of the modern state and economic development (3.3). Another key theme is the sources and outcomes of the many observed types of property rights – private, state, communal – as well as issues of open access. Elinor Ostrom's analysis of common pool governance among small, communal groups illustrates this range of institutional options (3.4). Notwithstanding this rich literature, there are many crucial unanswered questions (3.5).

3.1 Definition of property rights

Property rights have two meanings in economics: legal (or de jure) and economic (or de facto). New institutionalists have explored the formal institutions that define and enforce de jure rights (see e.g., Arruñada, 2003; Voigt, 2008; Voigt, Gutmann, and Field, 2015), and the informal institutions that constrain and support de facto rights (see, e.g., North and Thomas, 1973 [1999]; Ostrom, 1990; Greif, 2006).

3.1.1 Legal private property rights

Legal or formal property rights are assigned by the state and are "as old as human written records. From the Hammurabi code to the English common law the notion of legal ownership, or legal rights, to property is well defined" (Allen, 2000: 897). Legal rights have the advantage of third-party adjudication and enforcement (Barzel, 1989 [1997]), and are generally judged more secure than self-enforced or socially enforced rights. Both formal and informal property rights are credited with creating incentives to use resources in a more socially optimal way since owners internalize the benefits and costs of use (see Section 3.2). But there are other purported benefits to formal property rights, specifically: (1) they can be transferred at lower transaction costs to individuals motivated to use the resource most efficiently; (2) they reduce socially inefficient theft and conflict over insecure rights plus wasteful individual expenditures on protection (Trebilcock and Veel, 2008);[1] and (3) they are impersonal – they do not depend on who you are or your position in society – which is critical to the impersonal exchange underpinning modern society (North, 1990a; North, Wallis and Weingast, 2009).

3.1.2   Economic property rights

Economic property rights date from Alchian (1965: 818), who defined them as "the right to use goods (or to transfer that right)" so long as other property rights are not adversely affected. Legal rights are neither necessary nor sufficient for economic rights (Barzel, 2015: 719). They are not sufficient because you may have a legal right that is too costly to enforce (e.g., rights to a chunk of the Pacific Ocean) or norms may prevent exercising your rights, and not necessary because two owners can fully recognize and respect a boundary with a fuzzy legal basis and use the resource efficiently. Furthermore, some owners without legal rights may have de facto rights.

Studies suggest that formalizing informal rights increases owners' investment and the market values of assets. For example, Galiani and Schargrodsky (2010) found that legal title raised housing quality by 37 percent in a Buenos Aires slum, while Alston, Libecap and Mueller (1999) found that more secure titles increased land values by 36 percent in the Brazilian Amazon. Yet the picture is complicated. Sun and Ho (2016) cite case studies in Colombia, Mexico, Peru, and the US where legal titles did

---

[1]   See Coase (1960), Demsetz (1967) and Alchian and Demsetz (1973). Of course, society incurs costs for police, judges, etc. to protect private property rights.

not improve housing quality, increase property values or reduce poverty.[2] Payne (2001), Gonzalez (2009), and Sun and Ho (2016) document cases where squatters transferred and inherited property without legal title because they had the sanction of their slum community. Moreover, Ensminger (1997: 168) studied cases in Africa where the cost of formalizing an informal or customary right was more than the benefits.[3] This unsettled debate is the subject of much research.

3.1.3   Types of property rights

Besides the distinction between legal and economic property rights, Alchian (1965; 1993) described three types of property rights: private, state, and communal. Private and state property rights are the exclusive authority to determine how a resource is used and to exclude other users. Communal property rights are rights that can be exercised within a defined group of citizens or group members. As we shall show, Ostrom found that communal rights often are effective, but only where some exclusion is possible. Some scholars add a fourth type, distinguishing between communal property, where resources are restricted to a community under agreed rules, and open access (Hardin, 1968), where resources are available to all takers (Merrill, 2002). Assets are in the public domain or open access because the cost of excluding other claimants exceeds their value, in some cases because the asset values are low, but in others because the transaction costs of securing property rights are so high. These divisions are not clear-cut and are complicated by the many facets of property rights, their use, and exchange. For example, a landowner may lease the right to till the land to another person, while a third person or the state owns the right to traverse the land (Alchian and Demsetz, 1973: 17). We discuss the four types at greater length in Section 3.4.

---

[2]   Under some circumstances the causality may be reversed: Razzaz (1993) found that squatters in Jordan invested to gain de facto property rights since they assumed that the state would be less likely to demolish completed houses.

[3]   For additional studies of the sometimes adverse effects of converting informal to formal rights, see cites in Fitzpatrick (2005) and Trebilcock and Veel (2008).

3.2   Why are property rights so central to NIE?

The economic definition of property rights has profound implications. As Coase (1991 [2005]: 37) put it:

> what are traded on the market are not, as is often supposed by economists, physical entities but the right to perform certain actions ... it is obviously desirable that rights should be assigned to those who can use them most productively and with incentives that lead them to do so. It is also desirable that, to discover and maintain such a distribution of rights, the costs of their transference should be low ... this can come about only if there is an appropriate system of property rights (and that the rights are enforced).

For all these reasons, property rights are vital to three central NIE issues: (1) incentives; (2) transactions; and (3) contracts and firms.

3.2.1   Incentives

Property rights are central to NIE because they define incentives for resource use, production, investment, and trade. Holders of private property rights are motivated to safeguard and improve their property, as we saw with titles in Buenos Aires and the Amazon. The more complete their rights – the more the power to exclude others, to control the flow of resources from the asset and to transfer the asset – the stronger the motivation. Where property rights are completely defined, owners have incentives to invest in and provide private goods because they capture the net returns from doing so. Where such rights and related private returns are not feasible, private actors will underinvest, such as in infrastructure, aspects of health care, and national defense. These services hence are social goods due to the nature of the property right, and their provision depends upon government action. Property rights can also convey monopoly power; for example, some argue that patents on improved seeds contributed to industry consolidation (Matson, Tang and Wynn, 2012) and a decline in investment in innovation (Schimmelpfennig, Pray and Brennan, 2003).[4] Moreover, because we live in a world of positive

---

[4]   Recently the open-source model (putting ideas in the public domain) has challenged the arguments that traditional property rights are needed to motivate innovation. Open-source innovators may be more strongly motivated by intrinsic motivations: signaling their skills, educating themselves, acting altruistically, etc. (Maurer and Scotchmer, 2006). (A large literature

transaction costs, property rights are never entirely complete, while multiple owners dissipate the incentive effects. Incentive issues also loom when ownership and control are separate, as in large corporations, state-owned enterprises, and communal property.[5]

Another incentive issue arises because, in the absence of social or legal constraints, owners have little motivation to take into account the spill-over effects of their uses on others.[6] Coase called those spillovers social costs; most economists call them externalities. As we discussed in Chapter 1, Coase (1960) proposed that the affected parties might reach a bargain. Coase gives the example of a cattle raiser increasing the herd, which then damage a neighbor's crops. In the absence of legal liability, the cattle raiser might offer to rent the neighbor's parcel and keep it fallow or the farmer might agree to purchase fencing to keep out the roaming cattle. As we explore in Chapters 2 and 4, the feasibility of such contractual solutions depends on transaction costs as well as government regulation and legal precedents limiting owners' options. Multiple owners may not agree on solutions, an additional hurdle to bargaining. The transaction costs of bargaining are even higher for communal property, since no individual or sub-group of owners can exclude other users (Demsetz, 1967), although Ostrom described important exceptions (see Section 3.4).

3.2.2   Transactions

Transactions are about the transfer of rights to use a resource (see Chapter 2), which is central to the operation of a market economy. The more complete are property rights, the lower are transaction costs and the higher the gains from exchange (Allen, 2000: 898). This, combined with the incentive effects discussed above, explains why studies find stronger private property rights have beneficial economy-wide effects. For example, Acemoglu and Johnson (2005) find that income per capita and rates of investment are higher in countries where protection of property rights against expro-

---

deals with intrinsic motivation; see cites in Frey, 2001; 2017; Bénabou and Tirole, 2003.)

[5]   This issue in private corporations spawned a literature too extensive to cover here. See, for example, Berle and Means (1932); Arrow (1974); Chandler (1977); Fama and Jensen (1983).

[6]   State ownership is often exempted from regulation and can be a major source of externalities as with, for example, rampant pollution at US military bases (Hamilton, 2016).

priation or confiscation of returns by politicians and elites is stronger.[7] In a less formal treatment, North and Thomas (1973 [1999]) attribute the rising prosperity and productivity in Europe in the Middle Ages to increasingly stronger measures to protect property rights.[8]

Property rights affect not only the size of the economic pie, but also its distribution. North, Wallis and Weingast (2009) describe how elites in most societies except modern democracies restrict access to secure property rights solely to members of the dominant coalition. More inclusive property rights allow transfer of assets to owners who would use them more effectively, increasing returns and opportunities for exchange (see Box 3.1 on the experience of Poland and Ukraine).

Box 3.1   The history of property rights in Poland and Ukraine[9]

Poland and Ukraine have been economically and politically intertwined for over 650 years. Yet they diverged remarkably after the fall of communism in 1989 in Poland and in 1991 in Ukraine, despite very similar initial conditions (GDP per capita, urbanization and industrialization, infant mortality rates, etc.). Since its transition, Poland has grown rapidly, joined the European Union (EU) and the Organisation for Economic Co-operation and Development (OECD), and become an economic success story, while Ukraine has seen economic declines and two revolutions.[10] Despite "sharing a border, a similar language (mutually intelligible if spoken slowly), a long history of overlapping experiences and institutions and even substantially the same political institutional make-up post-1989, the two countries have emphatically *not* shared the same experience of property rights" (Hartwell, 2017: 143, emphasis in original).

Poland developed broad-based property rights defended by informal, small-scale institutions (such as village courts). "As early as 1348, 'a peasant ... had full rights of ownership of movable property, and in

---

[7]   See also Knack and Keefer (1995); Rodrik, Subramanian and Trebbi (2004).
[8]   See also de Long and Shleifer (1993).
[9]   Drawn from Hartwell (2017).
[10] Poland also benefitted from support from the EU and access to the common market.

some cases, he could buy, sell, and bequeath land"' (Kamiński, 1975: 267 quoted in Hartwell, 2017: 146). This tradition survived partitions, occupations, setbacks and the transition from communism. It was formalized through laws protecting private property rights and an independent judiciary. In contrast, Ukraine was never able to cultivate such diffusion of political power or broad-based property rights. During the transition, power stayed centralized in the communist dominated Parliament. Property rights remained insecure with episodes of land grabs, business expropriations, and a 19-year "temporary" moratorium on land sales.

> Recent events in Poland, including a move by the ruling party to politicize the Constitutional Court, shows that even established property rights may be tenuous in the face of concerted political opposition. In fact, the key lesson from history in both Ukraine and Poland is that diffusion of power can protect property rights, but ... the protection of both legal and economic property rights is a constant struggle ... (Hartwell, 2017: 156)

3.2.3   Contracts and firms

Property rights are central to another NIE preoccupation: contracts and firms. Coase (1960) and later Cheung (1983) described the firm's productive inputs as property rights. Following Coase, Cheung contended that the owner of a factor of production has the choice of "(1) producing and marketing goods himself, (2) selling his input outright [on the market], or (3) entering into a contractual arrangement surrendering the use of his input to an agent in exchange for an income" (1983: 3). As we know from Coase (1937), the owner's choice will attempt to economize on transaction costs (more on this in Chapter 5).

Labor is a special type of input, since human beings are not robots. Workers have discretion and information about their effort that supervisors lack which makes it costly to monitor effort (Alchian and Demsetz, 1973). Ways to address this information asymmetry through monetary and non-monetary incentives is the subject of a large literature,[11] including agency theory (see Chapter 1) and analyses of different contractual forms (such as wage labor, share cropping, and fixed rent in agriculture; see, e.g., Cheung, 1969b; Alston and Higgs, 1982; Allen and Lueck, 2003).

---

[11]   For an overview, see Miller (1992).

3.3   Institutions to define and enforce property rights

Throughout history, humans have devised creative ways to secure property rights that can be characterized as (1) informal and personal (such as a handshake); (2) semi-formal and semi-personal (such as community enforcement); and (3) formal and impersonal (such as written contracts and laws). The development of formal property rights enforced by courts and legal sanctions was a major innovation, even though informal and semi-formal mechanisms still predominate in contemporary economies (Macaulay, 1963). NIE has been preoccupied with the emergence of these formal institutions; see, for example, North and Thomas (1973 [1999], Greif (2006), North, Wallis and Weingast (2009).

3.3.1   Informal, personal

North, Wallis and Weingast (2009) argue that powerful elites used coercion, formed coalitions, made deals and eventually built governments to protect their property rights, not out of the goodness of their hearts, but because their rents were higher under social order than under endemic civil wars. Elites used the state to assure their domination of exchange by limiting non-elite access to markets or power. "Thus, property rights and legal systems have their origins in the definition of elite rights" (Shirley, 2008: 43).

In eras when information was scarce (and in similar circumstances today), merchants protected their property rights by transacting only with people whose reputation they or people they trusted knew. But relying solely on reputation limits transactions to personal exchanges. Social networks, such as religious, kinship or ethnic groups, extend exchange over wider circles and longer distances because network members can share their knowledge about reputations and enforce agreements by threatening to expel cheaters (North and Thomas, 1973 [1999]; North, 1990a; Greif, 1993). For example, Box 1.2 summarizes Greif's (1993) analysis of how Jewish Maghrebi traders during the Middle Ages used their common religion, ethnicity, language, and social ties to set up informal institutions to exchange information about which agents were trustworthy. Such networks expand trade beyond face-to-face exchange, but transactions are still restricted to members and require prior information on personal attributes. Nevertheless, Bernstein (2019) finds that such "small-world networks" have contract enforcement properties that effectively support trade among large numbers of traders at considerable distances in many modern industries.

3.3.2   Semi-formal, semi-personal

During the twelfth and thirteenth centuries, the "community responsibility system" allowed impersonal transactions across jurisdictions and over more than the lifespan of the individual merchant, according to Greif (2006). Semi-autonomous towns and cities or communes in Europe would stand behind the trustworthiness of their members when they travelled to markets (such as the annual Champagne fairs). If a commune member defaulted on a contract, the entire commune was legally liable and had to pay compensation or forfeit trading with that market (Greif, 2006). "By providing a way to enforce contracts with unknown merchants who were not part of any local social network but who were known in their home communities, commune enforcement was an intermediary between social enforcement and state enforcement, but it fell apart as towns grew and it became easier for cheats to pretend to be members of a commune" (Shirley, 2008: 27). Guilds, business associations, and the like similarly regulated members' behavior and had similar disadvantages. At a time when information was scarce and costly, it was difficult to add new members so transactions continued to be restricted to relatively narrow groups. Yet today, with information plentiful, these sorts of associations and groups continue to be important. For example, the New York Diamond Dealers Club signals and monitors reputations since members agree to submit all disputes to an arbitration board that has the power to fine, suspend, and expel members (Bernstein, 1992). Such associations are key to a secretive industry where "a handshake accompanied by the words *mazel u'broche* creates a binding agreement" for the exchange of millions of dollars in diamonds (Bernstein, 1992: 121). (See McMillan and Woodruff, 2000 for additional examples.)

3.3.3   Formal, impersonal

In Europe during the sixteenth and seventeenth centuries, the rules and customs of merchants were codified into the so-called Law Merchant enforced by town and city courts, the nobility or kings (North and Thomas, 1973 [1999]). North and Weingast (1989) describe how after the "Glorious Revolution" in England in 1688, the king could no longer arbitrarily issue monopolies, while the common law courts and Parliament, which were more favorable to property rights, became independent of the monarchy (see also Chapter 6). The effect was "a marked increase in the security of property rights" (North and Weingast, 1989: 804). There were other innovations as well; for example, Parliament issued patents. Previously, intellectual property was either not protected at all, requiring inventors to rely on secrecy, or protected through a monopoly subject to royal whims (North and Thomas, 1973 [1999]: 148–9).[12]

There are risks from relying on the law and courts, however. What stops the ruling faction from using government's power to confiscate the gains from exchange or even the property itself through quasi-legal means (such as confiscatory taxes)? The development of institutions to constrain the government from abusing its power contributed to the emergence of the modern state, as we discuss in detail in Chapter 6.

3.3.4   Public and private ordering

The development of property rights enforced by the government was a major innovation. However, legal rights are not usually embodied in laws but delineated in contracts (Barzel, 1989 [1997]). Moreover, property rights are predominately protected, not by resort to laws and the legal system (what Williamson termed "public ordering"), but through safeguards against opportunistic behavior built by the parties to the contract ("private ordering").

Private ordering affects the design of contracts and firms: the contractual parties will "realign incentives and embed transactions in a protective governance structure" to mitigate the contractual problems that would otherwise arise (Williamson, 2002: 438). We consider the issues around contracts in detail in Chapter 4.

---

[12]   Today, intellectual property rights cover increasingly intangible but valuable assets and are sometimes used in ways that deter innovation, as when patent holders buy and kill rival inventions. Hahn (2003) surveyed the literature on the effects of patents and found it "inconclusive" on whether stronger patents increase or decrease innovation (2). He concluded that "institutional factors ranging from the structure of research institutions to seemingly tangential laws appear to play a critical role in how patent policy gets translated into innovation and R&D" (39).

Public ordering is nevertheless vital:

> recourse to reliable courts for purposes of ultimate appeal, should private
> ordering efforts to resolve conflicts break down … reduces contractual risks
> that would otherwise deter exchange. Economies with better rules of the game
> will thus be able to support more complex and potentially hazardous interfirm
> transactions than will economies with less developed rules and/or less-reliable
> enforcement, ceteris paribus. (Williamson, 2002: 440 n2).[13]

Box 3.2 gives an example of how complexity affects the tradeoff between
public and private ordering.

Box 3.2   Private vs. public ordering in California's and Nevada's mines[14]

Mining in California and Nevada illustrates the importance of public
ordering for complex transactions (Anderson and Hill, 2004: ch. 6).
After gold was discovered in California in 1848, private ordering created well-defined and enforced property rights that were exchanged
through contracts. Despite some violence, miners generally adhered to
such cultural norms as the principle of first possession, justice through
majority rule, and trial by jury. With statehood, the private ordering
was codified in California's 1851 law (the Civil Practices Act) and
courts recognized the camps' "customs, usages and regulations" (114).
In 1866 the Federal Government further formalized many of the local
rules created through the mining camps' private ordering.

Initially, property rights over the gold and silver discovered in Nevada
in 1850 were also enforced through private ordering. However, Nevada's
major deposits were in deep veins, leading to numerous disputes over
surface versus subsurface rights, boundaries between veins, and rights
to follow veins branching off main veins, creating pressures for more
formal and permanent arrangements. Because of the complexity of establishing property rights to Nevada's rich underground veins and the
large returns to specialization in definition and enforcement of property rights, Nevada moved quickly to public ordering through the en-
actment of 178 statutes and a number of state Supreme Court verdicts.

---

[13]   See also Arruñada (2012a).
[14]   Based on Anderson and Hill (2004: ch. 6).

> Libecap (1978) shows statistically that Nevada's increased specificity of property rights was related to rising resource values and potential for conflict.

Thus far we have largely focused on private property rights, but the other types also present important issues for NIE research.

3.4   Private, state, communal, and absent property rights

We mentioned that property rights can be (1) private, (2) state, (3) communal (no member of a loosely defined community can exclude any other member), or (4) absent (open access, that is, in the public domain).

3.4.1   Private

We have been discussing private property rights as though they were static, but in reality, they are in flux because the costs of defining and enforcing property rights vary over time, across different institutional and economic settings, and with changes in technology. For example, although many farmers had legal title to their land in the Western US, their rights were not enforceable until the invention of barbed wire greatly reduced the cost of fencing to exclude grazing cattle (Anderson and Hill, 2004). The benefits of claiming property rights also fluctuate as asset values rise and fall with changes in technology, markets, and institutions (Barzel, 1989 [1997]). Individuals are constantly scrambling to buy, trade or steal property rights, and attempting to privatize rights in the public domain.

Given the constant vying for property rights, it is not surprising that they are sometimes the subject of prolonged conflict. Weak state institutions feed such conflict. For example, Alston, Libecap and Mueller (1999) describe how the government of Brazil adopted a policy of land redistribution but failed to provide enough resources, resulting in a woefully slow process. Landless peasants seized land, purposely designing their invasions to pressure the land reform agency and politicians to prioritize their demands for land redistribution. Landlords in turn appealed to local courts that typically evicted the squatters, resulting in a cycle of violence and wasted resources. While the Amazon is a story of private actors manipulating a weak government, in other cases there is no government enforcement and private actors fill the void. For example, the central government of the Democratic Republic of the Congo was too weak to enforce property rights over the minerals used for smart phones (such as tin, tungsten, and tantalum), and local militia groups asserted control over the mines (Parker and Vadheim, 2017). The situation was "highly imperfect" but stable until US regulation prohibited trade in these "conflict minerals," reducing the value to the militia of enforcing property rights. This, the authors contend, contributed to a surge in looting and violence.

Potentially private assets are sometimes in the public domain because their value is less than the cost of enforcing property rights. Changes in markets, technology, policy and other circumstances sometimes raise an asset's value above enforcement costs, prompting efforts to privatize the property right. For example, seeds used to be entirely in the public domain; farmers saved them from the harvest. After hybridization and later genetic modification, improved seeds gained value as a commodity to the point where the gains from privatizing the asset exceeded the transaction costs (Stein, 2005; Matson, Tang and Wynn, 2012; Ciliberto, Moschini and Perry, 2017). Commercial seed producers successfully lobbied the government for patent protection, which was granted in 1970. This privatization of seeds raised risks of concentration and monopoly power, with their potentially negative impact on innovation mentioned earlier (3.2).

3.4.2   State

State assets are in principle owned by the citizens of the locality and managed by the government as their agent. In reality, management of state assets is divided between bureaucrats and politicians with many objectives besides maximizing returns; these other objectives are theoretically the reasons for government ownership in the first place (Alchian, 1965). Moreover, the agents who manage state assets do not bear the same costs or benefits from their actions that a private owner might. Much of the empirical research on state ownership has focused on state-owned enterprises (SOEs) where government ownership is in direct competition with private. Government ownership of enterprises expanded from the

1930s until the 1980s, followed by several decades of privatization (for more on the reasons SOEs were created, see Box 7.3).

In support of Alchian's contention, empirical studies over decades (e.g., World Bank, 1995; IMF, 2020) have found that SOEs on average have consistently lower productivity and returns on assets than comparable private firms, although comparisons are difficult because SOEs and private firms often operate in different sectors under very different conditions.[15] SOEs may have lower returns because of their social goals, because governments require them to serve political ends or corrupt purposes or because their managers maximize their own utility with little oversight (see, e.g., World Bank, 1995). A large literature, well beyond the scope of this book, analyzes the theory and performance of SOEs and privatization.[16] Few studies, however, follow Coase's mandate and analyze the total costs and benefits of SOEs compared to alternative social arrangements. Notwithstanding the large literature on SOEs, there is ample room for further scholarship to address the gaps in our understanding, especially relevant since SOEs are more significant than ever in the global economy (see IMF, 2020).

3.4.3   Communal (common pool resources)

Confusingly, the term commons is used to refer to property subject to communal property rights as well as to open access. Commons include groundwater basins, wild fisheries, communal lands or waters, the earth's atmosphere, the Internet, and so on. Commons issues also arise in purely private domains, such as oil and gas fields where producers rush to maximize the economic value of their lease, rather than the reservoir as a whole, thereby wasting resources and raising costs (Libecap, 1998).[17]

Hardin (1968) famously stated that if no owner(s) can exclude others, users are motivated to use an "open access resource" first and fully, risking over-exploitation and eventual destruction in a "tragedy of the

---

[15]   For example, many SOEs are regulated utilities or large extractive firms with monopoly power.

[16]   See Megginson and Netter (2001) and Shirley and Walsh (2000) for surveys of the early literature and Megginson (2017) for contributions since 2000.

[17]   Unitization – assigning one unit producer to operate the entire field while the others take an agreed share in the rents – solves many of the commons problems but faces significant transaction costs to negotiate (Libecap, 1998).

commons." While Hardin characterized commons as open access, Elinor Ostrom argued that common resource ownership and management could sometimes successfully avoid over-exploitation if some exclusion is possible. She discovered through extensive field research that institutions in some local communities governed use in ways that were both economically and ecologically sustainable (Ostrom, 1990; 2009). Although the institutional details of sustainable governance varied greatly, Ostrom revealed a set of eight overarching design principles or best practices that were typical of enduring institutions.[18] Subsequently, Cox, Arnold and Villamayor-Tomás (2010) analyzed 91 empirical studies and found Ostrom's principles were "well supported empirically" (1), although Araral (2013) found some problems of confirmation bias, specification, multi-collinearity, and endogeneity in Cox's cases. Ostrom's ideas and her work at the Indiana Workshop spawned a huge outpouring of research (for a synthesis, see van Laerhoven and Ostrom, 2007). Examples include case studies of fisheries in Maine and Mexico; ancient irrigation in Nepal, Arizona, Spain, and the Philippines; forestry in India, Nepal, Guatemala, Colombia, and Bolivia; pasture in Kenya; wildlife in East Africa; public housing in China; and groundwater in California, among many others (see Araral, 2013 for citations).

Ostrom-style solutions can be hard to reach. As Ostrom put it, "When individuals who have high discount rates and little mutual trust act independently, without the capacity to communicate, to enter into binding agreements, and to arrange for monitoring and enforcing mechanisms, they are not likely to choose jointly beneficial strategies unless such strategies happen to be their dominant strategies" (1990: 183). Another hurdle: state authorities have to give at least minimal recognition to the communal institutions. Additionally, if the common pool resource is large, not bounded (making it especially hard to restrict access), heterogeneous in quality and high in value, and if the effects of over-exploitation are subject to dispute, the users will be unable to overcome the transaction costs

---

[18]   These included: (1) clear boundaries between the resource and the rest of the environment and (2) between users and non-users; (3) rules distributing costs proportional to benefits; (4) participation by most affected individuals in making and modifying rules; (5) monitoring by users and sanctions; (6) low cost, rapid local mechanisms to resolve conflicts; (7) minimal recognition by government of local users' rights to make their own rules; (8) for complex resources, arrangements organized in multiple, nested layers (Ostrom, 1990: ch. 3).

of negotiating institutions that fit Ostrom's design principles (Libecap, 2018). Because of these hurdles, many open access resources are not governed by institutions of the type anticipated by Ostrom, and we examine those next.

3.4.4   Absent or open access

Open access exists where property rights do not exist to constrain entry and use, leading competitors for rents to rush to exploit the asset, rampant free riding and waste of valuable resources in predation and defense, often followed by conflict and violence (Libecap, 2008a: 130). Property rights do not exist or are very incomplete because of high costs in definition and enforcement or political constraints. Araral (2013: 10) mentions examples:

> unsustainable pumping of groundwater in rural India ... and Northern China ..., the unabated destruction of corals and overfishing in the coral marine triangle – the so-called Amazon of the seas – in the southeast Pacific Ocean ... the massive degradation of the marine ecosystem in the South China sea ... the problem of collective action and hydro-hegemony in the Mekong River ... the unregulated use of the global atmosphere and oceans as a global sink.

For resources under control of one state, such as costal fisheries or interior lakes and groundwater, governments have tried regulating number of users or days of use, often with disappointing results, as Box 3.3 describes for Pacific halibut.

Box 3.3   Regulation vs. property rights in British Colombia halibut[19]

To reduce overfishing of halibut in the British Colombia fishing grounds, regulators restricted the number of licenses, then reduced the fishing season from 65 to 6 days. In response, fishers used larger vessels, increased crew, fished longer hours, and went out regardless of the weather, jeopardizing their safety. The effect was the opposite of the intention: fishers caught 50 percent more halibut in 1990 when the season was six days than in 1980 when the season was still 65 days (Grafton, Squires and Fox, 2000: 684). And with the entire harvest

---

[19]   This box is largely based on Libecap (2018).

caught in six days, most consumers could only get low-value, frozen halibut.

Transferable quotas were eventually issued for British Colombia's Pacific halibut to motivate fishers to follow more sustainable practices. Tradeable quotas only have value if fish stocks are vibrant (halibut stocks recovered), product quality is high and valuable (most of the harvest switched to fresh halibut), and costs are reasonable (the number of boats and size of crews shrunk, although average wages went up). However, the decline in owner-operators in favor of outside investors and its threat to coastal communities have led some to question the sustainability of the scheme (Edwards and Pinkerton, 2019).

Governments have also experimented with schemes that assign partial property rights, which in theory motivate users to preserve the resource – if the right is secure and valuable (in effect, it can be traded). Typically, governments cap total extraction and assign individual transferable quotas (ITQs) to users by grandfathering their present levels of use, as in Box 3.3. ITQs face sizeable transaction costs to win agreement among a diverse and large group of users over a high value, unbounded resource; they also raise difficult political economy issues. Issues of equity and consolidation make ITQs controversial and call for more Coasian analyses of the costs and benefits of feasible alternative social arrangements.

3.5   New research agenda

The NIE approach to property rights has opened a treasure trove of research possibilities. The debate over the benefits of formalizing rights is unresolved; pressing questions of state ownership continue to be current; and trends in intellectual property rights have opened new directions for study, such as open source. Additionally, many topics around the commons demand attention, including Ostrom-style solutions, ITQs, open access threats to environments and livelihoods and problems of newer commons, such as cyberspace. Parker (2018) suggests additional new and underexplored themes, for example: how new technologies or shifts in demand lead to the privatization of rights over resources in the public domain, such as the commercialization of sand or the non-use of pristine environments. Parker also calls for more attention to the anti-commons, where multiple individuals holding exclusion rights cause underinvestment, such as numerous small patents that have stymied pharmaceutical innovations. He also suggests more research on the political economy of privatization, such as constraints on property usage in Mexico that allow powerful politicians to reward influential constituents. These are only a few indications about what remains a very open and promising research agenda.

4   Contracts

Contracts are a cornerstone of new institutional economics (NIE) because contracts provide such powerful tools to organize transactions and coordinate partners. Williamson's pioneering paper (1971) proposed contracts as an alternative to vertical integration to address "transactional failures," launching a stream of theoretical and empirical research. NIE has played a central role in this effort, making "economics ... closer to being a 'science of contract' than a 'science of choice'" (Buchanan, 1975: 229).

A rich diversity of approaches came out of this initial impulse, but this chapter will necessarily focus on the NIE perspective. We first define contracts, explain why they are so central to NIE and how they differ from alternative approaches (4.1). We then summarize the strategic role of contracts in facilitating coordination and securing commitment and consider the limits they face, making most of them incomplete (4.2). We then turn to a landmark contribution of NIE to the economics of contracts: the exceptional combination of theoretical developments and empirical analyses that it has inspired (4.3). We conclude with remarks on how the NIE emphasis on making the theory of contract empirically relevant opens room for a rich and distinct research program (4.4). Throughout the chapter, we emphasize what we view as the hallmark of NIE's theory of contracts: a focus on contracts as (1) support to transactions in a world dominated by impersonal exchanges, which are (2) incomplete, raising issues of (3) *ex post* enforcement and adaptation.

4.1   Concept

Parties contract to govern complex transactions in order to organize the acquisition and use of assets (physical, human) and to secure the integrity of transactions supporting these activities (Joskow, 1988; Schwartz, 1992: 284; Gibbons, 2010)

4.1.1   The NIE concept of contract

Two perspectives on contracting dominate among economists. The "legalistic" perspective defines a contract as "an agreement between two or more parties creating obligations that are enforceable or otherwise recognizable at law" (Garner and Black, 2005 cited in Kornhauser and Macleod, 2013: 922).[1] The emphasis is on the formal dimension of contracts, with rights and obligations enforceable by a third party. Car rental contracts are an obvious example. Many economists endorse a more extensive perspective, considering all agreements among parties as contracts, whether these agreements are written or tacit, as long as they provide incentives to perform in a certain direction (Azariadis, 1975; MacLeod and Malcolmson, 1989). This raises particularly acute issues of verifiability and enforcement. A classical example, going back to Simon (1951), is labor contracts in which employees exchange partially implicit commitments with a firm employing their services for a certain period and under some "reasonable" terms (Azariadis, 1975: 1185).

In this book, we use a concept of contract rooted where these two approaches overlap, in the spirit of Macneil (1978) and Williamson (1985b; 1996).[2] A contract is hereafter understood as *a mutual agreement among well-specified parties determining transfers of rights and modalities to enforce these rights*. The main economic function of a contract is therefore to provide a framework within which transactions are organized and conducted.

---

[1]   "*A contract is a promise or a set of promises for the breach of which the law gives a remedy, or the performance of which the law in some way recognizes as a duty.*" (Restatement (Second) of contracts § 2 (Tent. Drafts Nos 1–7, 1973). Cited in Macneil (1974: 693).

[2]   See also Kornhauser and MacLeod (2013: 923); Lafontaine and Slade (2013: 959). Macaulay (1963: 3) provided a clear-cut definition of formal contracts as "devices for conducting exchanges" that involve two distinctive features: "(a) Rational planning of the transaction with careful provision for as many future contingencies as can be foreseen, and (b) the existence or use of actual or potential legal sanctions to induce performance of the exchange or to compensate for non-performance."

4.1.2   Why are contracts so central to NIE?

Analysis of contracts is a significant part of the NIE literature. But why do new institutional economists care so much about contracts? Why not leave this domain to legal scholars?

The fundamental motivation for this attention to contracts comes from their status as devices to organize and govern business activities (Macneil, 1974; Williamson, 1991; Gibbons, 2010). "The significance of contracts arises from their role in coordinating and securing economic activities when personal links and social norms can no longer provide enough guarantees to ensure that commitments will be respected" (Menard, 2004b, vol. 3: xvii). Besides facilitating coordination, contracts contribute to making commitments credible (more on this in 4.2), with formal contracts often helping to make relational agreements feasible (Klein, 2000a; Bernstein, 2015).[3]

4.1.3   What makes this theory of contracts distinct?

The NIE theory of contracts differs from alternative explanations through its emphasis on *ex post* enforcement and methods of adaptation, rather than focusing on the *ex ante* design of an optimal contract to efficiently govern non-contractible actions.

Specifically, it differs from Principal-Agent models (see Laffont and Martimort, 2002), which focus on the design of optimal incentive mechanisms embedded in contracts to overcome information asymmetries (arising from adverse selection or moral hazard) among contracting parties that have different utility functions. With its exclusive attention to the design of optimal contracts, this approach leaves no room for considering alternative modes of governance as possible solutions to these informational asymmetries. It also presumes the possibility of complete contracts with no renegotiations needed since it assumes the existence of

---

[3]   As Klein (2000a: 68) observed, "although Macaulay and others are correct in noting that many business relationships are self-enforced, transactors are not indifferent regarding the [formal] contract terms they choose to govern their self-enforcing relationships." Baker, Gibbons and Murphy (1994) may be the first to have introduced a model combining formal and relational contracting.

efficient institutions to enforce them: institutional failures are no part of this theoretical landscape.

Although the NIE and the "new property rights" (NPR) à la Grossman and Hart (1986; also Hart and Moore, 1988; 1999) were initially considered complementary, including by their "founding fathers," differences between NIE and NPR became progressively obvious. They diverge in their explanations of contractual incompleteness (more on this in 4.2). NIE emphasizes transaction costs as the main obstacle to the development and implementation of "optimal" contracts that could guide *ex post* adaptation; instead complementary modalities of governance are needed. NPR rather emphasizes the possibility of informational asymmetries not anticipated at the time the contract was agreed upon and that are non-verifiable by a third party (typically a court). In order to efficiently overcome these unexpected events, the NPR perspective advocates the design of a contract allocating *ex ante* property rights in a way that motivates parties to maximize their specific investments thanks to the control ownership confers over residual rights. This allocation of rights determines the bargaining position of agents in *ex post* renegotiations (Hart and Moore, 1988; 1990). The differences between NIE and NPR approaches to contracts lead to different research strategies. The NPR gives priority to building models of self-fulfilling contracts, making the internal organization of the firms or the institutional embeddedness of contracts irrelevant. In contrast, the NIE perspective gives priority to the analysis of *ex post* adaptation to unexpected events through alternative mechanisms of governance, opening a research strategy that has generated an abundant empirical literature (Box 4.1; more on this in Section 4.3).

Box 4.1   Contract design: theory and application

The economics of contractual agreements has become a big business, as the awards of Nobel Prizes to Oliver Williamson in 2009 and Oliver Hart and Bengt Holmström in 2016 attest. Williamson's approach, with its emphasis on *ex post* adaptation and enforcement, has been particularly successful in inspiring models that can be empirically tested (Whinston, 2001). Zanarone (2013) illustrates this with an interesting theoretical analysis of "contract adaptation under legal constraints" in franchising, followed by an application to car dealerships. The logic of the model and its test can be summarized as follows.

Let us assume a franchisor dealing with a set of N risk-neutral franchisees operating in a changing environment may need to adapt because of unprogrammed contingencies ("temporal adaptation") or because different franchisees face different local conditions ("local adaptation"). Franchisees benefit from laws (present in both the EU and the US) that protect them from "unfair and unequal treatment"; thus the allocation of decision rights and the structure of contract terms are subject to specific legal constraints.

The (logical) timing of the franchise relationship is captured in the following steps:

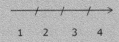

In t_1, the franchisor offers franchisees a long-term contract in which either (a) the franchisor has authority over a decision (e.g., choosing the design of stores), whatever the state of the world, or (b) the franchisees retain authority over that decision.

In t_2, a state of the world materializes that is observable by both parties. However, each franchisee faces a different cost of adapting to this state of the world.

In t_3, the parties negotiate over adaptation (possibly exchanging payments) given the allocation of authority defined by the initial contract (see t_1) and the legal constraints.

In t_4, the outcome is observable to all parties and the benefits are shared by the franchisor and the franchisees according to a share parameter specified by the initial contract.

The model illustrates the interdependence between the law and formal contracts and its impact on adaptation. It shows that by preventing the franchisor from negotiating different adaptation decisions with different franchisees (unequal treatment according to the law) and using her authority to extract payments from franchisees (unfair treatment), the law *creates* contracting frictions. That is, the law prevents adaptation decisions (e.g., changing the layout of stores) from being efficiently contracted *ex post* even though these decisions are verifiable. As a result, adaptation tends to occur too often (i.e., even if its cost to franchisees offsets the benefit to the franchisor) when the franchisor has author-ity to impose it, and too rarely under franchisee authority. Moreover, because of the prohibition against treating franchisees unequally, adap-tation tends to be too homogeneous (e.g., either all franchisees change store layout or none of them does). To gain flexibility, franchisors use self-enforcing relational agreements in the shadow of the law, while re-taining the formal authority to impose uniform adaptation when the franchisees are too tempted to renege due to externalities.

Testing this model through the case of franchise contracts between 19 representative car manufacturers and car dealers in Italy, Zanarone showed how anti-discrimination laws affect the design of franchise contracts, how the relational aspects of contracts prevent undesired judicial enforcement, and how the allocation of authority in incom-plete contracts is key to adaptation, all of which are consistent with the model's assumptions.

4.2   Contracts matter ... within limits

Notwithstanding nuances, there is a general agreement among NIE con-tributors that contracts play a key role in facilitating coordination and securing commitment, which requires particular attention to the costly conditions of enforcement and adaptation of contracts. Indeed, a central message of NIE is that the life of a contract begins *ex post*, once it is signed!

4.2.1   Coordination and commitment

"As Joskow (1985) emphasizes, the first question to be asked about con-tracts between firms is not which contract is chosen but rather why the parties are contracting at all" (Gibbons, 2010: 274–5). The question goes back to the influential paper by Macaulay (1963) who pointed out the importance beyond formal contracts of "handshake" agreements in doing business. The NIE literature suggests two complementary answers to the question of why parties are contracting.

First, contracts support coordination by: (1) providing *ex ante* incen-tives to transact and securing *ex post* returns; (2) creating "routines" in the decision-making process, thus facilitating convergence among parties when their agreement is required; and (3) reducing the risk of opportunistic behavior by imposing constraints on parties (deadlines, rewards, penalties, and so on), particularly when specific investments are at stake. A contract fulfills these functions by delineating an "acceptance zone" (Simon, 1951) within which parties can adapt to unprogrammed situations.

Second, contracts also contribute to making commitments credible, even in a one-shot transaction (with no repeated game), an issue that particularly matters in a world of impersonal exchange (Williamson, 1985a; North, 1990a; see also Chapter 1). Contracts build credible commitment by: (1) providing guarantees, typically under the form of "hostage" clauses (Williamson, 1985a: chs 7 and 8); (2) imposing constraints that delineate the decision-making domain (Lafontaine and Slade, 2013); (3) introducing "time" into the relationship among parties, for example through the promise of future deliveries, which partially relies upon and feeds reputation;[4] and (4) including clauses about enforcement, thus defining a built-in coercive dimension.[5] Contracts that make commitments credible facilitate transactions while limiting recourse to judicial dispute resolution, thus reducing transaction costs.

Box 4.2 Organizing transactions through contractual clauses

In his pioneering article, Macaulay (1963) reported interviews with 68 businessmen and lawyers representing 43 companies and six law firms, and he identified four types of provisions central to contracts that specify:

(a) purpose of the contract (the object of the transaction at stake),
(b) anticipated contingencies,
(c) defective performances, and
(d) legal sanctions.

The last two types of provisions usually remained relatively vague re-

---

[4]   "Contract is the projection of exchange into the future" (Macneil, 1974: 712–13).

[5]   Legal scholars refer to "coercion" as an essential dimension of contracts (Macneil, 1974: 704; Schwartz, 1992).

lying on "the opportunity for good faith" to solve disputes, which "are frequently settled without reference to the contract or potential or actual legal sanctions" (10). So why do contracts exist at all? Macaulay pointed out the role of contracts in facilitating communication among parties and promising gains that exceed the costs of contracting.

Over 50 years later, using a more quantitative methodology, Argyres, Bercovitz and Mayer (2007) reached similar conclusions. In a series of papers analyzing contracts involving high-technology firms, they identified contractual provisions that support the view of contracts as means to secure transactions and make commitments credible. Mayer and Argyres (2004) synthesized data collected from hundreds of contracts of high-tech firms operating in the aerospace, software and hardware, and IT services and concluded that five types of provisions, which largely overlap with those identified by Macaulay, are at the core of those contracts:

(a) The allocation of roles and responsibilities among parties,
(b) The allocation of rights to decide and to control,
(c) Devices for solving conflicts,
(d) Plans to deal with uncertainties, and
(e) Devices for organizing communication among parties.

4.2.2 Incompleteness: ill-defined contracts

Notwithstanding their positive role in coordinating and making commitments credible, contracts face limits: most contracts are incomplete. Williamson consistently endorsed Llewellyn's view of "contract as a framework," primarily implemented through private ordering so as to keep costly recourse to the courts as a last resort (Williamson, 2010: 679), a view that has percolated through recent developments in contract theory.[6]

---

[6] Revisiting the NPR model, Hart and Moore (2008) emphasized incomplete contracts as providing *ex ante* "reference points," thus opening room to *ex post* adaptation; however, adaptation would follow principles defined *ex ante* in what should be the optimal contract. Differently, relational contracts à la Baker-Gibbons-Murphy propose models dealing with incompleteness in relation to *ex post* opportunism (Baker, Gibbons and Murphy, 2008; Gibbons, 2010).

Two complementary approaches prevail among NIE contributors with respect to the sources of incompleteness, one focusing on behavioral assumptions, the other on environmental factors exogenous to the transaction. They converge in identifying non-contractible situations that limit what a contract can accomplish.

On the behavioral side, the combination of bounded rationality and opportunism (see Chapter 1: 1.3) may lead to ill-defined expectations because it is impossible for humans to collect and process information and build the knowledge required to predict perfectly (Simon, 1978; Schwartz, 1992: 272). On the environmental side, "un-programmed events" reveal missing contractual clauses or clauses that do not allow costless *ex post* adaptation.

Not surprisingly, legal scholars close to NIE have paid a lot of attention to these issues. The legal approach (well summarized in Schwartz, 1992: 278 sq.) sees sources of incompleteness in: (1) ambiguous or vague language; (2) "party inadvertence," when parties overlook a contracting problem (which can be related to bounded rationality); (3) the costs of creating contractual terms for solving a problem that exceeds parties' private gains from that solution; (4) clauses not enforceable by the legal system because of asymmetric information about behavior or because of situations that can be observed but not verified by a third party; and (5) situations in which parties rely on "anonymity," for example when wages are "pooled" for an entire category of workers in a labor contract, leaving room for discretionary adjustments through bonuses.[7]

Whatever the source(s), the result are non-contractibilities that motivate parties to adopt governance structures that fill in the blanks of contracts, for example, hierarchy in the firm or strategic centers monitoring joint ventures. This emphasis on the *ex post* consequences of contract incompleteness is at the core of NIE contributions to organization theory. As mentioned earlier, authors close to the neoclassical tradition focus instead on *ex ante* information problems due to unverifiable sources of unforeseen contingencies (Hart and Moore, 1990; Tirole, 1999), and their

---

[7]   Schwartz derives an interesting consequence of this typology, arguing that courts will have an incentive to "complete" the contract when conflicts arise from causes 1 to 3, but will rather adopt a "passive" position when causes 4 and 5 are at stake.

research strategy can be summarized as the quest for optimal contracts. Without denying *ex ante* factors of incompleteness, the NIE perspective remains skeptical about the idea of "optimal contracts." Detailed contractual definitions of rights, obligation and problem-solving procedures, even if possible, could imply absurdly high costs, amplified by the cost of their enforcement, a point already made by Goldberg (1976).[8]

Not all cases of incompleteness are consequential. Short delays due to a snowstorm in the agreed date for delivery of books I ordered through the Internet are unlikely to challenge my agreement to pay. The impact of "incompleteness becomes more severe as the number of features of a transaction (precision, linkages, compatibility) across which adaptations are needed increases and as the number of consequential disturbances that impinge on these features increases, which disturbances increase with the length of the contract" (Williamson, 2010: 680, n10).

4.2.3   Incompleteness: a problem or a solution?

Incompleteness of contracts confronts the contracting parties with a tradeoff between security and flexibility (Macneil, 1978: 853). A more complete contract might provide better safeguards against the risks of deficiencies or the opportunistic behavior of a partner, but reduces flexibility to adapt efficiently to contingencies (Williamson, 1971; 1975; Goldberg, 1976). As Crocker and Reynolds (1993) argued, contracting parties often face this tradeoff when they have to decide the degree of contractual completeness they find acceptable. Alternative modes of adaptation (e.g., through action by managers in a vertically integrated firm or by a "strategic center" in inter-firm agreements) might well be a second-best solution superior to the introduction of greater rigidity to make a contract relatively complete.[9]

---

[8]   The "measurement branch" of NIE, associated with Barzel (1982; 1989 [1997]), partially bridges the gap between *ex ante* and *ex post* perspectives. For example, the difficulty or even impossibility of measuring *ex ante* the quality of certain products (e.g., tomatoes in bulk) may feed *ex post* incentives to act opportunistically, leading to haggling, reneging or hold-up strategies that are hard to observe and above all cannot be verified by a third party, making contracts incomplete (Barzel, 1977; Klein, 1980).

[9]   Informal norms may also play a role. For example, high valued social commitment might alleviate the need for detailed contracts. Early on, this was

In the NIE perspective, incompleteness and transaction costs are tightly interwoven. Behavioral as well as environmental risks might push towards the introduction of more extensive safeguards, which increase rigidity and raise transactions costs. Symmetrically, costs may motivate parties to adopt incomplete contracts, often boiled down to a few pages, facilitating adaptation, but with higher exposure to opportunistic behavior and other contractual hazards. Empirical investigation is needed to assess the respective weight of these factors and the costs they generate. But what are these costs?

4.2.4   Cost of contracting

Contractual costs, a specific variety of transaction costs, differ depending on whether the focus is on *ex ante* negotiations or *ex post* implementation (Coase, 1937; Dahlman, 1979; Williamson, 1985a: 20–1).

Ex ante, the main contractual costs come from: (1) finding a reliable partner (or partners) that can provide needed goods and/or services, which involves information costs; (2) drafting, negotiating, and writing the final agreement (the infamous "ink costs," typically legal fees); and (3) setting *ex ante* conditions for implementation, including the creation of performance measures that are part of the reward function in an agency setting.

However, except for the rare case of complete and self-fulfilling contracts, the main costs emerge *ex post*, at the implementation and enforcement stage. (1) A contract may have been poorly designed or may not have properly anticipated contingencies and this maladaptation may require renegotiation. (2) Haggling may develop, leading to changes in contractual provisions and generating unexpected costs. (3) Monitoring the actual implementation of a contract may require setting up and running a specific governance structure (e.g., building a strategic center to monitor a joint venture). (4) Enforcing a contract might require the support of dispute resolution devices (e.g., arbitration or courts). (5) And renegotiation might fail, leading to breach of contract and raising the issue of how to implement penalty clauses.

---

the argument of Macaulay (1963). See also Zucker (1988), Williamson (1993), Greif (1993), Bernstein (1992; 2015).

Because most contracts are exposed to contractual hazards, parties to the agreement need to build safeguards as well as governance mechanisms in case hazards materialize. Typical solutions are: mechanisms to realign incentives (e.g., penalties for delays in delivery or breaching the contract); specialized organizations to address conflicts (e.g., international arbitrage); credible commitments of partners based on funds pledged as guaranties (hostage clauses) or on reputation (Klein, Crawford and Alchian, 1978; Williamson, 1985a).

Note that all the costs just mentioned are embedded in the drafting and monitoring of a contract. NIE contributors (e.g., Schwartz, 1992; Arruñada, 2012b) have pointed out that a significant part of these costs is "socialized," relying on institutions not connected to a specific contract but implemented by society to secure contractual arrangements, such as registration systems or specialized courts. These costs are "socialized" in the sense that they are external to the parties and supported by public administrations or private organizations (e.g., certifying organizations that oversee compliance with quality provisions stipulated in contracts).

NIE acknowledges the existence of *ex ante* costs. However, in contrast to the focus of alternative explanations on *ex ante* clauses that determine the *ex post* efficiency of a governance structure, NIE emphasizes the *ex post* capacity and costs of alternative contractual solutions to monitor hazards and facilitate adaptation to unprogrammed events.

4.3   Theoretical developments and empirical breakthroughs

Within this setting, the transactional approach to contracts blossomed in two directions.[10] On the theoretical side, recent developments emphasize the nature and role of relational contracts as a way to deal with incom-

---

[10]   As already mentioned, NPR (also called "incomplete contract theory") follows a different path with consequences for empirical analyses highlighted by Whinston (2001) and Gibbons (2005). Despite recent contributions suggesting possible complementarities (Lo, Ghosh and Zanarone, 2020), the gap remains between the NPR's focus on designing *ex ante* optimal contracts (Hart and Moore, 2008) and TCE's emphasis on the key role of *ex post* adaptation mechanisms (Gibbons, 2010).

pleteness. On the empirical side, a flow of empirical studies has substantiated the TCE approach, leading to its qualification as a "success story" (Williamson, 2000; 2010).

4.3.1   The strategic role of relational contracts

The emphasis on incompleteness may explain why the concept of relational contracts was and remains a hot research topic in NIE. Relational contracts deal with non-contractibilities through informal provisions and unwritten codes of conduct that are sustained by the value of future relationships (Goldberg, 1976: 427; Baker, Gibbons and Murphy, 2002: 39). They differ from complete contracts in that they are not enforceable by third parties. Their resilience depends on self-enforcing factors, for example, trust among parties or governance structures that minimize the temptation to renege. In a nutshell, relational contracts are blueprints that facilitate *ex post* adaptation without incurring dissuasive transaction costs.

4.3.2   Origin and development: the Macaulay-Macneil-Williamson filiation

Macaulay's pioneering article (Box 4.2) pointed out the key role of contracts in "*the creation of exchange relationships*" (1963: 4; italics by Macaulay), providing a "boiler plate" that allows adaptation to unforeseen contingencies. Parties develop relational contracts to avoid recourse to legal sanctions, because of their "desire to continue successfully in business and ... avoid conduct which might interfere with attaining this goal" (14). Building on these ideas, Macneil (1974; 1978), a legal scholar, introduced a typology of contracts depending on the choices between flexibility and rigidity, with relational contracts favoring flexibility through provisions to overcome conflicts and preserve the relationship, thus facilitating adaptation and "a joint creative effort" (Macneil, 1974: 739). Franchising or condominiums provide examples. Goldberg (1976) and Williamson (1979) picked up on this idea, contrasting relational contracts with contingent-claims contracts typical of pure market transactions in which the identity of parties is irrelevant, future disturbances relatively predictable and remedies narrowly prescribed, making these contracts observable by all parties involved and verifiable by third parties (typically a court).

Although regularly mentioned over the next two decades, the concept of relational contracts had to await influential contributions by Klein (1996) and Baker, Gibbons and Murphy (1999; 2002; 2008) to motivate a new stream of research. Building on a distinction between property rights, decision rights, and payoffs,[11] these contributors emphasized the role of relational contracts in inter-firm relationships. They also play a role within the firm, but this aspect remains largely underexplored (Gibbons, 2010; but see Gibbons and Henderson, 2012).[12] The argument for making relational contracts so central is in line with Williamson (1979): when outcomes can be observed only *ex post* and only by the contracting parties, while *ex ante* detailed specification would be prohibitively costly or even impossible, enforcement by third parties becomes irrelevant so that the resilience of the contract depends on whether the value of the future relationship is sufficiently large that neither party wishes to renege (Baker, Gibbons and Murphy, 2002: 40). Franchising provides a good illustration, with the need to make room for temporal as well as local adaptation (Zanarone, 2013 – see Box 4.1; also Lafontaine and Slade, 2013).

4.3.3   Empirical contributions

The NIE approach to contracts has generated such an abundant empirical literature, in-depth case studies as well as econometric tests, that a survey far exceeds the purpose of this chapter.[13] Here we only point out some key features of these contributions.

Initial empirical investigations started from Williamson's connection between types of contracts and the attributes of transactions (more on this in Chapter 5). The richness of these contributions has no equivalent in alternative approaches to contracts (Whinston, 2001; Lafontaine and Slade, 2007; 2013). Numerous case studies, initiated by Goldberg and

---

[11]   Public-private partnerships well illustrate the distinction, with public authorities holding property rights while substantial decision rights are in the hands of private operators who also have some control over the payoff. Payoff in the relational contract literature is broadly understood "as including everything that might affect an individual's experience of his or her job" (Gibbons and Henderson, 2012: 1353).

[12]   For surveys of the role of relational contracts in "hybrids," see Menard (2004a; 2013a) and Gil and Zanarone (2017).

[13]   See several chapters in Gibbons and Roberts (2013).

Erikson (1982), Joskow (1985), and Crocker and Masten (1985; 1988), have been followed by a stream of econometric studies showing the correlation between the attributes of transactions, particularly the specificity of assets involved, and the type of contracts and more generally the governance structures chosen.[14] A hallmark in that respect has been a series of articles by Joskow on the relationships between coal suppliers and electric utilities (Box 4.3).[15]

Box 4.3   An early test of the empirical relevance of the transaction cost approach to contracts

Following a statistical analysis of the contractual relationships between US coal suppliers and electric utilities (1985), Joskow developed a pioneering econometric study (1987) connecting the type of contracts implemented with the characteristics of the investments involved.

The article's central hypothesis was that "the variation in agreed upon duration of contractual commitments is directly related to variations in the importance of relationship-specific investments" (1987: 169). This relation was tested on a set of 277 US contracts negotiated in the years up to 1979 between coal suppliers and electric utilities. About 15 percent of transactions happened within vertically integrated firms, 15 percent through spot market purchases, and the remaining 70 percent through contracts lasting from one to fifty years. Building on Williamson's distinction between site, physical, and dedicated specificity, Joskow tested the following equation:

$$\text{Duration}_i = a_0 + b_1 \text{Quantity}_i + b_2 \text{Quantity}_i^2 + b_3 \text{Mine-mouth}_i + b_4 \text{Midwest}_i + b_5 \text{West}_i + u_i$$

with duration of a contract a function of the annual quantity to be delivered (Quantity_i^2 is to account for the cost of breaching a contract, likely declining over time as plants and mines are aging) and of the location of the mines, with Mine-mouth, Midwest, and West dummy

---

[14]   For surveys of this empirical literature, see Shelanski and Klein (1995), Klein (2005), Macher and Richman (2008).

[15]   Other pioneering articles using quantitative methods are Anderson and Schmittlein (1984) and Mulherin (1986).

variables taking the value 1 or 0 depending on the location of the coal mines involved, measuring the regional effects relative to contracts for Eastern coal. Site specificity matters a lot since the characteristics of mines (and their number) differ significantly according to the region, so that both technological characteristics of the physical assets and the volume of dedicated assets vary accordingly (the 1985 article explored this aspect extensively). Three different estimations and checks for control variables confirmed the Williamsonian hypothesis that the variations in the importance of relationship-specific investments deeply affect the type of contract adopted, with long-term contracts allowing more relational adaptation.

A second wave of empirical studies, developed mostly over the last decade, focuses on the nature and properties of relational contracts. These studies pay particular attention to the dimensions defining relational contracts: their informal components (see the pioneering paper of Bernstein, 1992 on the diamond sector); the assessment of the expected value of a sustained relationship (e.g., Macchiavello and Morjaria, 2015 on Kenyan rose exports); and the interaction between the relational contract and formal governance (e.g., Gil, 2013 on the movie industry).

These are only illustrations of the fruitfulness of the NIE approach to contracts as an inspiration for empirical studies.

4.3.4   Institutions matter: the embeddedness of contracts

Another issue taken on board by NIE and largely ignored by alternative approaches is the institutional embeddedness of relational contracts, and more generally of all types of contracts. As already noted by Macneil, contracts could not develop without institutional support, typically laws regulating property rights, support rooted in "moral, economic, social, legal" conditions that are external to the contracting parties (1974: 746 sq.).

In this respect, NIE pays particular attention to the role of the judiciary,[16] assuming that all contracts operate "in the shadow of the law" (Kornhauser and Mnookin, 1979; Kornhauser and MacLeod, 2013).

---

[16]   This goes back to Coase (1960). See also his analysis of the role of the polities (1947; 1959).

Indeed, by considering most contracts incomplete this approach opens room for the role of "intermediaries," typically courts, to resolve disputes (Schwartz, 1992: 272). However, referring disputes to courts has implications for transaction costs (Schwartz, 1992: 277-8). On the one hand, using the judicial system is costly, with part of these costs incurred by the society that subsidizes the system. On the other hand, courts' intervention might minimize the costs of adaptation generated by incomplete contracts (e.g., the cost of renegotiating) by supplying legal rules that routinize solutions to recurrent problems (e.g., by establishing "precedents").

However, non-contractibilities make conformity to some clauses unverifiable and expose legal litigation to judicial arbitrariness and errors. This is a fundamental rationale for relational contracts as a means to circumvent judicial flaws and costs. But self-enforcement might also fail, requiring dispute mechanisms external to the parties to overcome conflicts and maintain the relationship. Consider arbitration (Rubin, 2005: 216 sq.). Arbitrators have presumably an advantage over courts in their superior knowledge of the industry and the conflicting parties. However, arbitration can be intrusive, revealing information to the opposing party and/or competitors that might be detrimental to one or both parties. Public authorities may provide other means to limit contractual hazards, for example through laws supporting credible commitment or through intermediate, meso-institutions (e.g., a regulatory agency), delivering guidelines that frame parties' behavior (Kunneke, Menard and Groenewegen, 2021: ch. 2). Alternatively, this role could be assumed by private institutions, particularly when public institutions are weak. The role of the Middle-Age merchant guilds in securing contracts among parties is an example (Greif, Milgrom and Weingast, 1994; Greif, 2006). Other factors more difficult to capture analytically can also support contractual agreements. For example, the identity of parties may enforce credibility, whether rooted in their personal reputation ("trust"), or in their membership in a well-identified community (e.g., a family or a social or even ethnic group; Ben-Porath, 1980; Ouchi, 1980; Bernstein, 1992, etc.) or more generally their participation in third-party institutions with shared beliefs and values (Greif, 1993; also Box 1.2 about the Maghribi traders).

Further exploration of these institutional dimensions and their role in determining the costs of organizing transaction through contracts remains high on the research agenda of institutional economists.

4.4   Conclusions

New institutional economists pioneered the development of theoretical and empirical investigation of contracts in organizing transactions. The success of the contractual approach far exceeds the new institutional contributions. Nevertheless, the NIE perspective differs from other influential approaches, as we have pointed out, leading to different research agendas. By concentrating their attention on the design of optimal contracts *ex ante* to deal with unexpected contingencies through incentive mechanisms (the Principal-Agent approach) or through the appropriate allocation of property rights (the NPR approach), these models leave little room for considerations of alternative modes of governance and/or the institutional setting within which contracts operate.

By contrast, although they acknowledge the existence of contractual clauses that influence *ex ante* efforts to be delivered by agents,[17] NIE contributors primarily concentrate on the risk of *ex post* opportunism and the conditions of enforcement of contracts. The focus therefore shifts to the modalities to organize the *ex post* governance of contractual relations within this context of incompleteness and to secure the continuity of the relationship among parties despite contractual hazards and "unprogrammed adaptation" (Williamson, 1971: 120; and 2010: 680). Indeed, a major lesson from NIE is that contracts cannot do it all! For example, firms cannot be understood exclusively as a (perfect) nexus of contracts. They have internal rules, which Williamson summarized under the idea of "forbearance." Through the attention paid to governance issues and the diversity of possible solutions to deal with contractual hazards, NIE has pushed further the intuition of Macneil (1974; 1978) about the existence of a variety of contracts and their embeddedness in different types of organizations within which transactions can be decided and efficiently conducted. We now turn to this aspect of the NIE research agenda.

---

[17]   For example, simple piece rate contracts in some manufacturing or sales activities.

PART II

Institutional layers

5 The organization of transactions

The numerous ways in which economic actors organize their activities are at the very core of market economies. Mainstream economics has long ignored these fundamentals, boiling down the analysis to a narrow view of markets as price mechanisms and firms as production functions. New institutional economics (NIE) radically changed this perspective, treating the variety of organizational solutions as key to understanding how economies work. Parallel to and interacting with the "Northian" branch, which focuses on the role of institutions operating at the macro-level, and particularly those institutions relating to property rights (see Chapter 3), the "Williamsonian" branch addresses Coase's challenge to explain why there are alternative solutions to market arrangements and what differentiates them (Coase, 1937).

Transaction costs economics (TCE) à la Williamson, a core component of NIE, provides tools to better understand the variety of organizational arrangements that form the backbone of modern economies. Although this chapter pays almost exclusive attention to the analysis of those arrangements through which economic transactions are decided and conducted, identified as organizations in TCE, it must be said upfront that TCE influence has gone far beyond economics, permeating management (see Anderson and Gatignon, 2005), as well as political science and other social sciences (see Chapters 6 and 7; and Menard and Shirley, 2018).

Initially developed as an answer to Coase's question about the rationale for the tradeoff between markets and firms (Williamson, 1975; 1985a), TCE was later extended to include the large set of transactions embedded in inter-organizational arrangements called "hybrids" (Williamson, 1996: ch. 4; Menard, 2004a). This theoretical breakthrough turned the mystery of "firms" as economic black boxes, then prevailing in micro-economics and industrial organization, into an open and intense field of research. This chapter boils down hundreds of contributions that made TCE part of the hard core of NIE by demonstrating that market economies rely on a variety of ways to organize transactions. Identifying and characterizing these arrangements and understanding why one might be preferred and/ or preferable to another has been and remains an active field of research.

Our chapter summarizes this conceptual revolution[1] by reviewing the "generic forms of governance" (Williamson, 1996: 93) that support transactions, that is: markets, hierarchies, and hybrids (5.1), recalling the key factors that make each choice transaction specific and that explain why one organizational solution is (or might be) preferred to another (5.2), and providing guidance to the huge empirical literature on organizations that this approach initiated (5.3). We conclude with a short overview of challenges that could inspire future research (5.4).

5.1   Organizing transactions: the variety of solutions

The very existence of organizations comes from the benefits expected from the division of labor (Coase, 1998). However, these gains come at a cost. In his famous discussion about the respective merits of manufacturing versus a purely decentralized production of pins, Adam Smith (1776 [1976]: ch. 1) asked: how can agents take advantage of specialization without losing the benefits of cooperation? Indeed, the division of labor implies the decomposition of tasks, which creates problems of coordination among interdependent agents, and is the origin of the search for cost-minimizing organizational solutions. Specialization also creates problems of cooperation, which is about motivating parties to overcome their diverse and sometime conflicting interests in order to efficiently exploit their complementarities. The two dimensions are distinct: even when cooperation prevails, coordination remains an issue.

5.1.1   Concept of organization

TCE investigates the variety of organizational answers to the question raised by Adam Smith, with particular attention to the factors that might explain the choice of one solution over another, that is, to rely on markets in certain cases, an integrated firm in other cases, or some other alternative, such as joint ventures, franchising, and so on, in still other cases.

---

[1]   For a view contrasting alternative approaches, see Gibbons (2005; 2010).

This approach refers to a certain conception of organizations. The term "organization" has many different meanings. North (1990a: 5) defines organizations as "groups of individuals bound by some common purpose to achieve objectives," thus covering a very wide range of situations. For TCE "organization" is a more focused concept. Williamson (1985a: 387–8; 1996: 378; also Allen, 2000: 900) defined organizations as those *governance structures through which transactions are drafted, negotiated, implemented, and conducted with a view to minimizing costs*. In other words, organizations designate the set of possible modalities among which decision-makers can choose to govern the transfer and usage of rights over goods and services in order to benefit from the division of labor.[2]

This concept of organization is grounded in NIE's golden triangle of transaction costs, contracts, and property rights. Parties choose how to transfer rights with a view to minimize transaction costs. Contracts provide the means for organizing these transfers in contexts of imperfect information and limited knowledge, fixing a framework for future actions and restraining opportunistic behavior. Well-defined property rights and the institutions for defining and enforcing them support the organization of transactions (*ex ante*) and provide incentives for transactors to fulfill their commitments (*ex post*).

5.1.2   Alternative organizational solutions

Following Coase's advice to analyze what differentiates organizational arrangements, Williamson (1996: ch. 4; 2010: 681) and followers propose three criteria: (1) the intensity of incentives; (2) the strength of "administrative command and control"; and (3) the supportive contract law regime. Underlying these criteria is the "main purpose of economic organization" (Williamson, 2010: 679) which is to provide modalities to adapt to transactional hazards.

---

[2]   Referring to Commons, Williamson characterizes organizations as "governance structures," "governance [being] the means by which *order* is accomplished in a relation in which potential *conflicts* threatens to undo or upset opportunities to realize *mutual* gains" (1996: 12; italics in original). Kunneke, Menard and Groenewegen (2021: ch. 2; see also Chapter 1) propose the term "micro-institutions" to better capture the diversity of these governance structures while pointing out that they are all institutionally embedded.

These criteria characterize three "generic forms of governance." (1) Markets provide particularly strong incentives since parties can appropriate net receipts; minimize the use of administrative command as a coordinating device by operating through the decentralized price mechanism; and rely in the last resort on external enforcers, typically courts, to monitor bad players and solve disputes. (2) At the other end of the spectrum, "hierarchies" (also called "unified organizations," typically firms) provide weaker incentives than markets, rely on administrative command-and-control to coordinate, and mobilize a specific contract law regime ("forbearance," defined below) in which private internal order provides the "ultimate court of appeal." Lastly, (3) hybrids cover the whole set of inter-organizational arrangements that transfer rights across fixed firm boundaries (e.g., long-term inter-firm contracts, leasing, licensing arrangements, franchising, and so on – see Coase, 1988a: 55; Menard, 2004a; Baker, Gibbons and Murphy, 2008). Hybrid arrangements are market-like in some aspects of the three criteria, hierarchy-like in other aspects (Makadok and Coff, 2009). They remain distinct in that they require specific mechanisms of governance in order to secure simultaneously coordination and cooperation in a context of partially shared rights (Menard, 2013a; Reuer and Devarakonda, 2016). Table 5.1 synthesizes these characteristics.

Table 5.1   Main characteristics differentiating the generic forms of governance

MODES OF ORGANIZATIONS / CRITERIA	MARKETS	HYBRIDS	HIERARCHIES ('unified organizations')
INCENTIVES (Intensity)	**Strong**	**Semi-strong**	**Weak**
ADMINISTRATIVE COMMAND-AND-CONTROL	**Weak**	**Semi-strong**	**Strong**
CONTRACTUAL LAW REGIME	**Strong**	**Semi-strong**	**Weak**

Source: Adapted from Williamson (1996: 105).

These generic forms of governance contain a wide variety of subcategories, which illustrate the richness of organizational arrangements in market economies. For example, beside the traditional micro-economic differentiation of market structures (Varian, 1992), Chandler (1966; 1977) suggested a distinction between "unitary" firms (U-form) and "multidivisional" firms (M-form) (Williamson, 1975: ch. 8; 1985a: ch. 11; Alchian and Woodward, 1988),[3] while Menard (2004a; 2013a) and Baker, Gibbons and Murphy (2008) pointed out the variety of hybrid arrangements. However, there is a consensus among most new institutional economists that these subcategories fall under the criteria that identify the generic forms.

5.1.3   Contractual regimes

Differences in contractual regimes across these forms illustrate how these distinctions apply. TCE hypothesizes that "each generic form of governance – market, hybrids, and hierarchy – needs to be supported by a different form of contract law" (Williamson, 1996: 95; see also Chapter 4).[4] Accordingly, (1) market arrangements rely on "contingent-claims contracting," comprehensive contracts that connect parties through legally binding rules and formal provisions and are self-liquidating once the transaction at stake is completed; in the last resort the identity of the transactors does not matter. (2) By contrast, "the implicit contract law of internal organization is that of forbearance" (1996: 98): within the general rules that apply to all types of organizational arrangements (e.g., liability law), the judiciary routinely confirms the rights of hierarchies to operate through "fiat" and act as their own courts of ultimate appeal. Finally, (3) hybrids depend on inter-organizational agreements to monitor shared rights among entities that remain legally distinct, operating through contractual agreements that provide a highly flexible framework ("an elastic contracting mechanism") to face unanticipated disturbances while maintaining "the entire relation as it has developed ... [through] time" (1996: 96). In hybrids, autonomy of parties is preserved and arbitration is favored over courts for solving disputes.

---

[3]   Other structures characterizing unified organizations have been discussed (e.g., Mintzberg, 1983; Aoki, 1990).

[4]   Recent developments in the theory of contracts likely require nuance in this sharp distinction (see Chapter 4, Section 4.3, and Box 5.3).

Contingent-claims contracts have been and remain the favorite domain of investigation among mainstream economists. With the notable exception of the analysis of incentives, contractual arrangements within firms remain a relatively neglected domain in economics (Gibbons, 2010). Many scholars follow the argument that a firm is a "nexus of contracts" with no significant difference from other contractual arrangements (Alchian and Demsetz, 1972; Fama, 1980).[5] However, most NIE contributors, building on Barnard (1938) and Simon (1951), consider the contracts ruling relations within the firm as distinct. A close examination of legal rules about employment contracts forcefully substantiates this argument (Box 5.1).

Box 5.1 Labor contracts as a distinct form of contract

Masten (1988 [1991]) analyzed the distinctiveness of labor contracts, contrasting the way law treats commercial and employment transactions. A careful examination of "the case law governing the relationships between employers and employees" versus independent contractors shows substantial differences.

1. The two types of contracts diverge with respect to duties and obligations. The employer has the right to control the manner in which work is performed and not only its outcome, as would be the case with an independent contractor. Symmetrically, the employee commits to reveal relevant information to the employer and to be "loyal," not taking advantage of his/her position in a way detrimental to the employer. There are no comparable obligations with regard to contractors. The counterpart for the employer is that he/she remains liable for any harms caused to a third party in the employee's fulfillment of his/her duties.
2. The firm can implement mechanisms to enforce these duties, for example, the employee may be held liable for damages to the employer's business due to "disloyal" or uncooperative behavior (e.g., transferring the knowledge acquired in a firm to a competitor) and/or internally defined sanctions may be imposed

---

[5]   The often cited statement by Alchian and Demsetz (1972: 777) pretends that the relationship between an employee and his/her employer is by no means different from the power of a consumer "to manage and assign his grocer to various tasks."

should the employee deviate from the contractual agreement. By contrast, in a commercial contract the independent contractor can hardly be accountable for "lack of loyalty" and remains free to take advantage of capabilities developed in the course of the contractual agreement.

3. Termination procedures differ between commercial and employment contracts. The motivation to breach an employment contract may arise from factors (such as "indolence," "disrespect," "insubordination") that "would not constitute an actionable cause for discharge of a commercial contract" (205). However, proving "bad faith" to breach a labor contract is challenging, and the firm will rather rely on internal procedures. By contrast, fixed obligations are routinely embedded in a commercial contract, with sanctions (e.g., penalties for delays) usually specified and implementable by a third party, typically courts.

In sum, an essential feature of employment contracts is the discretion left to the employer to direct the employee's behavior (Simon, 1951: 294), with the internal hierarchy being "the ultimate court of appeal" as long as labor and contract laws are respected.

Lastly, the key role of adaptability in contracts regulating hybrid arrangements launched an extensive literature on relational contracts (Baker, Gibbons and Murphy, 2002: 58 sq.; and Section 4.3) and the additional governance mechanisms used to deal with the combination of shared rights and autonomy that characterize these arrangements (Williamson, 1996: 97; Menard, 2004a; 2013a). Joint ventures, strategic alliances, and other inter-firm agreements fall under this category.

5.2 Tradeoffs among organizational arrangements

By providing an inclusive model of the variety of ways to organize transactions, NIE greatly enriched economists' vision of how market economies operate. The conceptual tools supporting the transaction cost model allow scholars to differentiate among markets, hierarchies, and hybrids. It also provided a way to understand the tradeoffs among these arrangements, thereby establishing TCE's strong reputation for empirical relevance.

5.2.1   Tradeoffs: key determinants

New institutionalists look at the tradeoffs among organizational arrangements through the lens of attributes characterizing a transaction (Williamson, 1985a: ch. 3). The underlying hypothesis is the "discriminating alignment hypothesis": "transactions, which differ in their attributes, are aligned with governance structures, which differ in their cost and competence, so as to effect a (mainly) transaction cost economizing result" (Williamson, 1996: 41).

Three transactional attributes are especially relevant: (1) the specificity of assets required for a transaction to be completed, (2) the uncertainties specific to a transaction that could plague its organization, and (3) the frequency with which a transaction is repeated. *Specificity of assets* (see Box 5.2) designates the value of investment in a transaction that would be lost or significantly downgraded in any alternative use. *Uncertainty* can be generated by the behavior of parties to the transaction, difficulties in assessing value (the "measurement" issue) or organizational deficiencies; it can also result from exogenous factors (see below). Lastly, the *frequency* of transaction impacts knowledge about its properties and about the reliability of the parties involved, thus reducing fixed costs per transaction. Equation (5.1) expresses the expected impact (positive or negative) of an increase in each of these independent variables (AS, U, F) on the dependent variable (TC):

$$TC = f\left(\underset{+}{AS}, \underset{+}{U}, \underset{-}{F}\right) \tag{5.1}$$

The core hypothesis of TCE is that positive variations in an independent variable (indicated by the underlying sign) generate hazards leading to the adoption of costly safeguards to secure the transactions and the continuity of the relationship among transactors (a negative sign suggests the opposite effect). The next step is to establish a correlation between the resulting transaction costs and the organizational arrangements (see below).

Part of the assessment of the impact of the independent variables relies on their measurement, a crucial ... and notoriously difficult exercise (Masten, Meehan and Snyder, 1991; also 5.3). Most empirical studies capture these attributes through proxies.[6] For example, the "asset specificity" variable has been broken down into components (Box 5.2) facilitating the development of econometric tests that played a significant part in making TCE a "success story" (Williamson, 2010).

Box 5.2   Different dimensions of asset specificity

Asset specificity refers to investments associated with a specific transaction that are not redeployable to alternative transactions, or redeployable only at high cost (Klein and Leffler, 1981; Williamson, 1985a: ch. 2).

Williamson initially identified four types of specificity:

1. Physical specificity refers to characteristics of the equipment needed for a certain transaction, such as specialized trucks for collecting milk or rail cars for transporting chemical products.
2. Site specificity is about the location requirements of an indispensable asset. For example, the high volume of energy required to produce aluminum explains the strong incentive to locate plants close to electricity suppliers.[7]
3. Dedicated assets concern the volume of investments required to satisfy the demand associated with a certain transaction. Investments required for aligning the technology for producing electricity to the quality of coal available is a case in point.
4. Human assets refer to the know-how or other specific qualifications that a job may require for specific transactions, such as the sales force or specialized engineers in high-tech industries.

Two more types of specificity were added later (Williamson, 1996: 105), to incorporate lessons from empirical tests:

---

[6]   There are some rare attempts to measure transaction costs directly at the macro-level (e.g., North and Wallis, 1986); or the micro-level (e.g., Benham, 2005).

[7]   The classical debate between Klein and Coase about the decision of General Motors to integrate Fisher Body largely focuses on the role of this variable. Pro- and con-arguments are discussed in several articles of the *Journal of Law and Economics*, 2000, 43 (1).

5. Brand names, since they require specific investments from contracting parties to secure the reputation of the product. Private voluntary standards in the agrifood industry are an example.
6. Temporal specificity, which relates to the necessity for intertemporal coordination for the achievement of certain transactions. The sequence of transactions in naval shipbuilding illustrates this (Masten, Meehan and Snyder, 1991).

Throughout all these cases, what really matters is the "specificity" involved (Gibbons, 2010), since specificity creates mutual dependence among transacting parties and raises the possibility of hazards that could threaten the realization of the transaction at stake. Associated risks may explain the predominance of this variable in empirical tests of the alignment between transaction costs and organizational arrangements.

Before summarizing the logic underlying these tests, we consider other factors that contribute to transaction costs and are often neglected or subsumed under the attributes mentioned above. These factors are exogenous in that they develop independently of the characteristics of the transaction at stake. Behavior rooted in social norms, weak or inadequate institutions, or unexpected environmental events are key examples. At the micro-level, behavior that can secure transactions and lower their costs is a case in point. The reliability of handshake agreements (Macaulay, 1963) or commitments framed by values shared by traders belonging to a specific community (Bernstein, 1992; Greif, 1993) illustrate this. By contrast, fuzzier contexts, for example black markets (Turvani, 1997), likely feed higher risk of opportunistic behavior, pushing transaction costs upward. At the macro-level, ill-defined property rights and/or weak enforcing institutions likely make the appropriation of rents potentially more conflictual, generating extra transaction costs (Williamson, 1971: 120–1). By contrast, social norms embedded in specific institutional settings (e.g., rules ordering the Champagne Fairs – see Chapter 3) might well determine trust, making contracts and their enforcement less costly (Williamson, 1971; Arrow, 1974; Oxley, 1999; see also Box 8.4). The credibility of courts plays a similar role (Schwartz, 1992; Hadfield, 2005). Finally, unexpected events, for example, climate warming, require adaptation that opens door to haggling, generating higher transaction costs.

This combination of factors embedded in a transaction (its attributes) or in elements that go well beyond a specific transaction determines what Coase (1991 [2005]) called the "institutional structure of production." They shape the tradeoff among "institutional arrangements" (North, 1990a), also qualified as "micro-institutions" (Menard, 2018; Kunneke, Menard and Groenewegen, 2021: ch. 2).

5.2.2   Modeling the tradeoffs

The initial model developed by Williamson (1985a: 90 sq.), which remains a key reference in empirical studies, is based on the attributes of transactions listed above.[8] Assuming that competition (even within bureaucracies) motivates cost-minimizing strategies, the model hypothesizes the following relation between transactions' attributes and organizational arrangements.[9] (1) The more specific the assets, making substitutes increasingly hard to find and creating mutual dependence among transactors, the more exposed they are to contractual hazards and to the risk of "hold-up" (the *ex post* appropriation of the quasi-rent: Klein, Crawford and Alchian, 1978; Alchian and Woodward, 1987: 114; Carson, Madhok and Wu, 2006: 1059).[10] The resulting high cost of using markets leads decision-makers to implement strong contractual safeguards or even choose merger or acquisition. (2) Similarly, the higher the uncertainty surrounding a transaction, the more incentives parties have to develop contractual safeguards or even integrate, especially if this combines with specific assets. (3) Lastly, higher frequency has ambiguous effects on organizational choices. On the one hand, it facilitates observability and reduces fixed unitary costs, which may favor organizing transactions within the firm. On the other hand, it allows standardization and benchmarking, which may make it advantageous to rely on market competition among suppliers (Williamson, 1985a: chs 2 and 4).[11]

---

[8]   TCE had to wait for Oxley (1999) to have an empirical study introducing explicitly the role of exogenous factors (see Box 5.4).

[9]   These assumptions are from the point of view of a decision-maker who must acquire inputs through a specific transaction. Similar reasoning can apply for the holder of these inputs (Cheung, 1983: 3).

[10]   Coase vigorously challenged the significance of "hold-up" as a motivation for organizational choices and it remains a controversial issue in NIE (see Coase, 2000; Freeland, 2000; Klein, 2000b).

[11]   Referring to Williamson (1979), Gibbons (2010, n9) alternatively argues that "frequency provides a boundary condition separating private order-

Assuming that transactors follow a cost-minimizing strategy, the core hypothesis is summarized by the "discriminating alignment hypothesis" (Williamson, 1996: 41, 371; Tadelis and Williamson, 2013: 168): parties have an incentive to choose the organizational arrangement (market, hybrid or hierarchy) best aligned with the observed attributes of the transaction at stake in order to minimize transaction costs. Figure 5.1 encapsulates the resulting research strategy, implemented in hundreds of empirical tests (see Box 5.3)

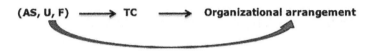

Figure 5.1   The logic underlying empirical tests

This emphasis on the role of transaction costs as a determinant of organizational choice[12] does not preclude the role of production costs (see Williamson, 1979: 245–6). However, it makes TCE radically different from previous approaches that considered technology, which underlies the "production function," as the core explanation for the existence and properties of the firm. This reduces the role of managers to an algorithm combining factors of production and leaves inter-organizational agreements unexplained. Conversely, the transaction cost approach makes the role of decision-makers (managers, entrepreneurs) and the tradeoffs among the variety of organizational solutions central to understanding the micro-level of economies. It also helps explain why all organizational solutions are imperfect: they all suffer from (different) "transactional failures" (Williamson, 1971: 112–13), which open the door to misalignment between the attributes of transactions and the mode of organization

---

ing (where only the parties themselves are involved in governance), which is efficient for high-frequency transactions, from trilateral governance (where a third party such as an arbitrator is involved in governance), which is efficient for low-frequency transactions."

[12]   Note that the alignment principle can be considered as a positive principle (explaining the observable choice of a specific arrangement) or a normative one (identifying which solution should be preferred).

chosen, something that cannot be explained without considering the role of decision-makers (Gibbons, 2010; Gibbons and Henderson, 2012).

The initial transaction cost model and related tests focused almost entirely on the tradeoff between "markets" and "hierarchies." TCE had to await the later contribution of Williamson (1996: ch. 4) to extend the original model to hybrid arrangements, while a new wave of theoretical contributions (Gibbons, 2005; Baker, Gibbons and Murphy, 2008) promoted the analysis of contractual regimes and the role of property rights as central to the tradeoffs. Box 5.3 briefly synthesizes these developments.

Box 5.3 Enriched tradeoffs synthesized

In essays integrating post-Williamsonian developments, Menard (2013a; 2014; 2018) proposed the following representation of the extended transaction cost model of organizational choices.

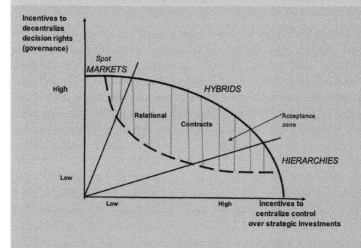

Figure 5.2   The fundamental tradeoffs

In this figure, the horizontal axis indicates the intensity with which *property rights* are centralized, which depends on the strategic nature of the investments involved (from low to high). The vertical axis captures the intensity of decentralization (or "delegation") of *decision rights*, again from low to high, which correlates with the uncertainty affecting the transaction at stake. Combining these two dimensions delineates the domain of organizational arrangements (or "micro-institutions"). The upper curve designates the "possibility frontier," above which the organization of transactions becomes unsustainable (e.g., uncertainty surrounding the transaction at stake is just too high, and/or property rights are too ill-defined). The lower curve delineates the domain under which transactions rarely develop except under pure arrangements (pure "spot" markets, pure "hierarchies"), which are rather exceptional forms (contrary to their prevalence in standard neoclassical theory).

In a world in which there are non-contractibilities, most transactions are organized within the space delineated by these two curves. This "acceptance zone" (Simon, 1951) is the domain of relational contracts: contracts that provide only a framework, a blueprint within which parties to the transactions adjust mutually through managerial coordination (Baker, Gibbons and Murphy, 2008; Menard, 2013a). This is also the domain where *hybrid arrangements* tend to prevail.

5.3   The booming industry of empirical tests in TCE

In contrast to the neoclassical "production function" view of the firm, TCE creates the opportunity to investigate the variety of organizational arrangements and the rationale behind the tradeoffs among alternative solutions. The result is a remarkable stream of empirical studies. Summarizing these contributions far exceeds the scope of this chapter (see partial surveys in Shelanski and Klein, 1995; Menard, 2004a; 2013a; Joskow, 2005; Klein, 2005; Macher and Richman, 2008). Instead, we emphasize some fundamental orientations and challenges in this literature.

5.3.1   Preliminaries: measurement as key to a comparative analysis

The research strategy adopted by TCE raises measurement problems. Economists using other strategies face similar problems, for example in measuring "opportunity costs." However, the TCE measurement issues deserve particular attention since measurement is so crucial for the comparative approach promoted by NIE. Proxies are routinely used (see Box 5.2) to circumvent the obstacles of direct measurement (Barzel, 1982).

Testing "discriminating alignment" requires estimating the comparative advantages of alternative solutions or, more relevant for empirical studies, the efficiency of the organizational arrangement actually chosen compared to possible alternatives (Gibbons, 2005: 220 sq.).

Masten, Meehan and Snyder (1991) nicely summarized the methodological difficulty at stake. Let us assume that I^* designates the preferable solution between organizing a specific transaction in-house (I°) or through the relevant market (I^m). This choice could be expressed as:

$$I^* = \begin{cases} I^\circ \text{ if } G^\circ < G^m \\ \\ I^m \text{ if } G^\circ \geq G^m \end{cases} \tag{5.2}$$

with G° and G^m the respective costs of these modes of governance as determined by the vector X and Y of the attributes of this specific transaction. We have:

$$G^\circ = \alpha X + \varepsilon$$

$$G^m = \beta Y + \mu \tag{5.3}$$

The problem in empirical estimation is that the available data are about the chosen form, not the putative one.[13] Although different methods can partially circumvent this problem, as shown by the authors in their examination of the organizational choices made by a naval shipbuilding company, this is not a trivial exercise. Indeed, it requires collecting data about what motivated a firm to choose in-house or markets for its supply, data that are often considered "business secrets" or are simply not available (Gibbons, 2010; also several chapters in Gibbons and Roberts, 2013).

---

[13]   "At best, one observes costs for the institution chosen so that direct comparisons with costs of alternative institutions are impossible" (Masten, Meehan and Snyder, 1991: 2).

Notwithstanding these difficulties, pioneering articles showed the possibility of identifying proxies that allowed empirical tests of the tradeoff between markets and hierarchies, opening the way to a huge number of contributions. Among them are Monteverde and Teece (1982) who tested the role of asset specificity in the "make or buy" tradeoff in the automobile industry; Masten (1984) who estimated the role of specific investments in the organization of the aerospace industry; Anderson and Schmittlein (1984) who showed the role of human assets and uncertainty in the tradeoff between integrating a sales force within the firm or outsourcing to independent salesmen; and Joskow (1985; see Box 4.3) who explored the impact of site specificity on the choice of contractual arrangements between coal mines and electric utilities. Numerous developments followed, partially reviewed in the surveys mentioned above.

5.3.2   Taking hybrids into consideration

The bulk of initial contributions focused on the "make or buy" tradeoff. Later, the integration of hybrids into the theoretical framework led to "make," "buy," or "make jointly" and to a renewed flow of empirical investigations into the tradeoffs among these alternative arrangements.

One stream of research explores the properties differentiating the governance of hybrids from markets and hierarchies, particularly with respect to the mechanisms of control, the allocation of rights, and the incentives at stake (see 5.1). The goal is to better capture the comparative advantage of "going hybrid." There are a wide variety of case studies from that perspective, particularly on strategic alliances, supply chains, joint ventures, and so on (Menard, 2004a; 2013a), and on franchising and its puzzling combination of independent franchisees and company-owned outlets (see Lafontaine and Slade, 2007).

Another stream of research focuses explicitly on the tradeoff itself, looking at the relation between the decision to choose hybrids over alternative solutions and the attributes of the transaction at stake. Two articles initiated research in this direction. Menard (1996) explored the choice between alternative modalities of contractual agreements through the example of the French poultry industry, showing the key role of a governing authority complementing contracts in most cases. Oxley (1999) tested the impact of institutional features on transaction costs and the resulting choice between equity-based and contract-based arrangements in situations involving technology transfer or joint research (Box 5.4).

Box 5.4   The tradeoff among alternative inter-firm agreements

Oxley (1997; 1999) provided empirical tests showing that the combination of transaction costs and institutional features (namely, intellectual property protection) were key determinants of organizational choices in inter-firm agreements in high-tech sectors.

Her 1997 article adopted a standard strategy in TCE, but innovated by extending the analysis of the tradeoff to hybrids. She identified three types of inter-firm alliances: unilateral agreements, for example, licensing; bilateral agreements, for example, joint research projects; and equity-based alliances, for example, joint ventures. Using an extensive data set (CATI) about technological transfers linking US and non-US-based firms that covered over 9,000 cooperative agreements in different technological domains, she tested the impact of transaction attributes on organizational choices. She showed that ill-defined property rights bred uncertainty and complex transactions (as when multiple technologies are involved) that challenged rent appropriation and prompted a preference for equity-based agreements above other solutions.

In 1999, she went further, analyzing the impact of "institutional parameters," such as weak versus strong enforcement of property rights, on organizational choices. Using the same data set (CATI) to assess the attributes of the transactions at stake and an index of intellectual property rights (IPINDEX) to capture variations in their protection (e.g., contract enforcement), she showed that US companies tend to choose equity joint ventures with local partners, a form close to hierarchy, when they intend to enter foreign markets with weak intellectual protection. By contrast, in countries in which rights are well defined and protected, they instead adopt contract-based alliances such as licensing. Checking several control variables (cultural distance, societal trust, education, political risks, etc.) confirmed this result.

Both articles confirm the fundamental assumption of TCE: contractual hazards, whether caused by the attributes of a transaction and/or by its institutional environment, are crucial for understanding organizational choices.

In the numerous empirical studies that followed, TCE showed a clear advantage over alternative explanations such as the "new property rights" approach or agency theory when it comes to empirical tests (e.g., Whinston, 2001; Lafontaine and Slade, 2007; Menard, 2013a; Gil and Zanarone, 2017; Argyres, Bercovitz and Zanarone, 2019).

Notwithstanding these developments, much remains to be done to better understand the conditions under which hybrids might outperform markets and integrated firms. Another puzzling issue, already raised by the case of franchising, is the existence of "plural forms" in which decision-makers opt for simultaneously managing similar transactions through different organizational arrangements (Bradach and Eccles, 1989; Bradach, 1997; Menard, 2013b; Menard, Schnaider and Saes, 2018).

5.4   Conclusions

The NIE theory of organization focuses on the transaction as the basic unit of analysis and treats the cost of implementing a transaction to its final execution as key to explaining the existence and properties of alternative modes of organization and the tradeoffs among them. In that respect, it differs from agency theory, which primarily examines incentives, that is, the way principals can induce agents to behave according to their own interests; the "new property rights" approach, which centers on ownership and the related allocation of decision rights for understanding relationship-specific investments; and the resource-based and evolutionary views, which mainly focus on how integrated organizations differ in dealing with their environment, especially through the development of routines and know-how.

Part of the success of the TCE branch of NIE in comparison to alternative explanations comes from the persuasive and insightful empirical tests it has generated. Nevertheless, there are many exciting topics still requiring investigation. The characteristics that make governance different across alternative organizational arrangements remain hot topics. Motivating factors, besides monetary incentives, that support cooperation and explain the comparative advantage of a specific solution need more systematic exploration. The study of relational contracts and their different role in alternative organizational arrangements is a promising avenue (Gibbons, 2010; 2020). Also, the question of how technology interacts with and contributes to the choice of a specific organizational arrangement remains a largely open question, as illustrated by the challenging impact of technological changes in the energy sector (Kunneke, Menard and Groenewegen, 2021: ch. 5). And novel forms of organization spawned by the new technologies of information and communication offer new opportunities for investigation through the TCE theoretical lenses.

Many other prospects for future research could be mentioned.[14] The rich set of concepts and tests developed in NIE has already had a major impact on the development of the economics of organization and its orientation. It has shed light on the variety of pillars that support transactions and generate the richness and complexity of modern market economies. It has also introduced new perspectives with respect to regulatory issues, an aspect we discuss in Chapter 7.

---

[14]   Numerous examples are provided in our companion book (Menard and Shirley, 2018).

6   State and legal institutions

For new institutional economics (NIE), the effectiveness of state and legal institutions is a determinant of economic development and societal well-being. Effective state and legal institutions define and protect property rights, control violence, provide for defense and social order, establish impartial and equitable rule of law and deliver necessary infrastructure and services. Since such institutions are the subject of extensive analyses in other disciplines, we first examine what distinguishes NIE's approach and makes it especially useful for understanding how these institutions operate in the real world (6.1). This deep interest in understanding how institutions operate in reality is combined with curiosity among new institutionalists about the origins of good institutions, prompting research on how today's modern and effective state and legal institutions first emerged in medieval Europe (6.2). NIE's drive to understand effective institutions also led to a large literature on balancing sufficient power to meet social needs with constraints against abuse, rendering government credible to investors and accountable to citizens (6.3). Researchers agree that this tricky balance between power and constraints requires an impersonal, impartial, accessible, and effective legal system, but disagree over issues, such as the role of legal origins and even how to measure rule of law (6.4). Moreover, some countries, notably China, have managed to grow rapidly with few formal constraints on state power and weak legal systems (6.5). Finally, we consider the many mysteries and new frontiers that remain despite all this productive research (6.6).

6.1   What distinguishes the NIE approach?

Just as neoclassical models take a functioning market economy as a benchmark, they also presume effective political and legal institutions. NIE, however, takes none of these for granted. Instead, the new institutional literature explores the complex origin and operation of state and legal institutions and their flaws (e.g., North, 1990a; North, Wallis and Weingast, 2009; Acemoglu and Robinson, 2012; 2019).

A starting point for neoclassical theory was government as "a benevolent guardian, hampered only by ignorance of proper economic policy as it seeks disinterestedly to maximize a Benthamite social welfare function" (Krueger, 1990: 172). Public choice theory put an end to some of that reasoning, but later theories of government agencies still tend to regard public administration as somehow separate from politics (Moe, 2013). With the advent of NIE, however, researchers began to use transaction cost and agency theories to analyze political bargaining and to understand politicians' incentives when they design political structures, interact with each other, and delegate implementation to bureaucracies (Moe, 1984; 1990; Weingast and Marshall, 1988; Weingast, 1989; more on this in Chapter 7).

Other political models, such as political economy and public choice, also examine state and legal institutions, but NIE theories assume that at the heart of puzzling socio-economic phenomena are previously unexplored institutional details. Thus, a new institutionalist's first instinct is to ask: do distortions in formal rules or informal norms and their enforcement explain the phenomenon in question? In considering the state, a new institutionalist will first identify the main actors (e.g., voters, legislators, executives) and institutions (e.g., constitutional provisions, parliamentary rules) relevant to decision making and explore the previously unexamined incentives and information asymmetries at work. We can see this in the ways that new institutionalists explain the origins and functioning of the institutional arrangements that underpin modern and effective states.

6.2　Origins of modern states and legal systems

Numerous social scientists have analyzed what Mokyr (2002) called "the enduring riddle of European development." The NIE perspective has focused on the rise of institutions in medieval Europe that underpinned emerging markets, encouraged technological advances, and curbed abuses by increasingly powerful and consolidated nation states. We can only briefly summarize this literature here.

North and Thomas (1973 [1999]) and Greif (2005; 2006) attribute the gradual transformation of medieval Europe's feudal societies ruled by unaccountable monarchs and nobles into predominately effective and democratic governments to the gradual emergence of an intricate web of institutional innovations. North and Thomas describe how Europe's expanding urban population, discovery of the new world, and emergence of nation states motivated merchants to exploit new trading opportunities and reduce their transaction costs by developing credit instruments, capital markets, standardized measures, dispute resolution mechanisms, and so on. Greif describes the spread of "self-governing, interest-based, and intentionally established organizations," such as the community responsibility systems described in Chapter 3, which produced new rules and altered beliefs (Greif, 2006: 389).[1] In his view, the traditions of corporatism, individualism, and self-government over time led to modern corporations and the bottom-up, organic formation of modern states and impersonal rule of law, starting in the Dutch Republic and England. In Chapter 3 (3.3), we described how property rights evolved into increasingly impersonal and formal rights enforced by governments as part of this process.

These authors also argue that such institutional innovations took hold in Europe precisely because of the weaknesses of its ruling coalitions, especially in England. North and Weingast (1989) describe how England's "Glorious Revolution" in 1688 ushered in a larger role for Parliament in fiscal decisions, made it hard for the king to call or dissolve Parliament at will and curtailed royal prerogatives and subordinated them to common law.[2]

Acemoglu and Robinson (2016; 2019) see Europe's transformation as a bottom-up rather than top-down or elite-driven process. In their view, increasing state capacity was balanced by pressure for wider political participation from common people bound together by social norms and organizations that developed long before the modern democratic state was formed. Acemoglu and Robinson (2019; see also Greif, 2006) credit

---

[1]   In Greif's view, the Catholic Church played a role by weakening kin-based social structures such as clans and tribes, thus contributing to norms of individualism.

[2]   North and Weingast's (1989) famous explanation for the Glorious Revolution has been disputed. Pincus and Robertson (2014) agree that the critical change in England's institutions that North and Weingast described did happen, but attribute the changes less to a de jure rewriting of the rules and more to a de facto shift in the balance of power between the monarchy and the merchants.

the inheritance of state institutions from the Roman Empire and participatory norms and institutions from Germanic tribes as supporting this fortuitous balance between central authority and common people.

A complementary narrative stresses changes in beliefs and ideas.[3] Mokyr (2002; 2016 [2018]) argues that slowly emerging beliefs in the transformative power of useful ideas and innovation coevolved with Europe's changing institutions and was spread by expanding literacy, urbanization, universities, printing presses, journals, and places for discussion (reading clubs, coffee houses, salons, etc.). Mokyr (2016 [2018]: 179) argues that Europe's polycentric political environment coexisted with a "transnational Republic of Letters" that created a competitive market for ideas, motivating and supporting intellectual innovation. These factors "chipped away at the old social order, worldview, and dominant belief system" (Shirley, 2008: 142).

6.3   State power balanced by constraints and accountability

The NIE vision of an effective state is one with sufficient power to protect property rights, wage wars, enforce laws, and provide public services. Such a state has a monopoly over violence, exercised by a competent military and police force under political control that maintains internal order, prevents theft and fraud, enforces contracts and defends against external threats (see North, Wallis and Weingast, 2009). States without sufficient, consolidated power over the means of violence risk disorder and instability, if not anarchy, and those without civilian control over the military suffer frequent military interventions. An extreme example of this is the Democratic Republic of the Congo with "a poorly disciplined, poorly trained military force that regularly preys on the civilian population, commits human rights abuses, and is incapable of protecting the

---

[3]   McCloskey (2006; 2010; 2016a; 2016b) challenges the institutional argument and argues that it was the erosion of society's disdain towards commerce and economic activity that gave the bourgeoisie increased freedom to innovate, brought liberty and dignity to commoners including the bourgeoisie, and led to the "Great Enrichment" after 1800. She stresses changes in ideas, rhetoric, ethics, and ideology.

country's borders from foreign incursions or ensuring domestic security" (Kaiser and Wolters, 2013: 98). But how to prevent a state with sufficient power from using its power arbitrarily to confiscate assets and infringe on rights?

The NIE's answer is institutions to empower a mobilized and informed civil society (see, e.g., North and Weingast, 1989; Weingast, 1997; North, Summerhill and Weingast, 2000; North, Wallis and Weingast, 2009; Acemoglu and Robinson, 2012; 2019). North, Wallis and Weingast (2009: 24) describe a "double balance": open access and entry to organizations in the economy balanced by open access and entry to politics and vice versa. In this model, open access to the economy fosters a large and varied set of organizations formed by many groups competing in the market who become politically active when their interests are threatened (North, Wallis and Weingast, 2009: 25). Open access in politics encourages competitive political parties and allows citizens to form many kinds of civic organizations (unions, business associations, lobbying groups, political parties) to coordinate and advance their interests. To achieve this double balance, access needs to be combined with widely held beliefs in inclusion and equality for all citizens, and institutions supporting rights, such as rule of law; a free press; constitutional guarantees of freedom of expression, religion, and right to assemble; and judicial and bureaucratic mechanisms to enforce these rights (North, Wallis and Weingast, 2009: 115). Acemoglu and Robinson (2012; 2019) similarly argue that a strong state must be balanced by a strong, mobilized society able to "shackle the leviathan" and keep the system in the "narrow corridor" where liberty prevails. They view this as a continual struggle between state and society, as Hartwell (2017) argues for Poland (see Box 3.1). As usual, the devil is in the details of how the many competing interest groups can overcome collective action problems and organize. Moreover, citizens may organize to protest state abuses but they also organize to pressure for state policies favoring their narrow interests. Bardhan (2016: 867) argues that to promote investment and harmony a state must have "the capacity to make credible commitments in the face of pressures from diverse interest groups."

NIE has probed deeply into the institutional arrangements that curb abuses, hold politicians accountable, and promote policies to benefit broad social interest. Here we consider three: elections, federalism, and curbs on executive power.[4]

6.3.1   Electoral systems

Much of positive political science deals with elections; what distinguishes NIE is its constant exploration of previously unexplored institutional details and their effects on outcomes. Thus, new institutionalists have focused on specific electoral rules, how votes are counted, how parties are organized, and the like.

Elections are not the same as democracy; indeed, one important research question is why many non-democracies choose to hold elections, and why elections do not necessarily reinforce democracy. A large literature describes how functioning democracies require not only wide access to the franchise and competitive elections free of coercion and suppression of voting, but also that incumbents who lose elections have incentives to step down and those out of power to eschew force (Przeworski, 1991; Mittal and Weingast, 2010). NIE again emphasizes the motivation and capacity of like-minded citizens to act in concert against political leaders who violate the rules (North, Wallis and Weingast, 2009; Acemoglu and Robinson, 2019).[5]

For citizens to be effective, Keefer (2011; also Acemoglu and Robinson, 2012; 2019) argues, they must be able to form organizations that overcome the collective action problems identified by Olson (1965) by providing information and means to hold leaders and members accountable and prevent free riding.[6] "Citizens who can act collectively can more easily hold challengers accountable for promises to pursue different policies than badly-performing incumbents, to provide public goods, to refrain from expropriation, or to reward civil servants for conscientiously implementing policies in the public interest" (Keefer, 2011: 6). In his view, programmatic political parties can play this role because they produce policy

---

[4]   Space does not permit us to cover all the NIE literature on constraints. We omit, for example, independent government agencies, such as central banks (although we take up independent central banks in Chapter 7).

[5]   Chapter 7 deals with issues of collective action and non-democracy in more detail.

[6]   There is a large literature on this subject; see cites in Keefer (2011) and Chapter 7.

programs that voters can monitor and discipline members who undermine party goals. Otherwise, according to Cruz and Keefer (2015), politicians will more likely rely upon client-patronage systems to win votes, motivating them to undermine reforms that might curb their patronage opportunities and to provide weaker oversight of the executive branch for the same reason. This was a problem in Argentina (see Box 6.1), as in many other countries. Acemoglu and Robinson (2019: ch. 11) assert that unaccountable states with rudimentary capacity that rely on patron-client relations to maintain power are a widespread legacy of colonialism (they cite Argentina, Colombia, Ghana, and Liberia among others).

Box 6.1   Argentina, the devil is in the details

Argentina illustrates how specific institutional arrangements can undermine macro rules. Argentina's institutions are superficially similar to the US (federalism, separation of powers, bicameral legislature). At the end of the eighteenth century, Argentina's per capita income was higher than the US. But by 2007, Argentina had suffered reoccurring economic crises with massive inflation and public debt; half its population lived in poverty.

Spiller and Tommasi (2007) describe how Argentina's political and economic institutions contributed to this deterioration by hindering cooperation and long-term solutions to economic problems:

1. Argentina's federal system undermined fiscal accountability, since the national government raised most revenues but the 24 provinces made most expenditures. Voters overwhelmingly reelected provincial governors who were best at extracting rents from the common central pool. Provincial party leaders relied on "patronage, pork barrel politics, and clientelism" to mobilize voters and dominate local and national politics (79–80).
2. Provincial party bosses had disproportionate power over federal legislators. Under Argentina's proportional representation system, they controlled a candidate's rank on the party list, which often determined whether they were elected.[7] Legislators, therefore,

---

[7]   Seats in the legislature are distributed to each party broadly in proportion to the party's total vote and then allocated to candidates based on their position on the list. Voters select a list, not an individual on the list.

had little incentive to curb the nation's fiscal deficits if that meant cutting funds for their province and alienating local party leaders.

3. On average national legislators served only one term, many preferring to return to more consequential roles in provincial politics, contributing to their preference for short-term benefits over long-term solutions.

4. Executives and cabinet officials also changed frequently, leaving the underpaid and demotivated bureaucracy without consistent leadership. Adding to the instability, presidents faced weak constitutional, judicial, or budgetary constraints on unilateral actions and often reneged on previous agreements.

Finally, Argentina's institutional configuration and clientelistic norms gave civil society few incentives or means to constrain political actors. To the contrary, some non-government organizations (such as business groups and unions) also tried to maximize their short-term benefits.

Supportive institutions, such as programmatic political parties, and a mobilized and organized civic society, are absent in many so-called democracies, which may explain why empirical studies find democracy has ambiguous effects on growth and inequality. One 2005 review concluded: "the net effect of democracy on growth performance cross-nationally over the last five decades is negative or null" (Gerring et al., 2005: 323). Some analysts suggest that democracy allows middle- and lower-income voters to redistribute income from the rich to themselves (an argument usually attributed to the median voter theorem of Meltzer and Richard, 1981), which could discourage investment and harm growth. North, Wallis and Weingast (2009: 142) counter that open access orders characterized by "inclusion, equality, and impersonality" are more likely to produce widely accessible public goods such as mass education, financial and transportation infrastructure and social insurance programs, than soak-the-rich transfers.[8] In support of this idea, and in contrast to other analyses, Acemoglu and Robinson (2019: 51) find a sizeable and significant causal effect of democracy on growth, which they hypothesize is because democ-

---

[8]   In support of this contention, they point to studies showing that unions and businesses cooperated in the design of Western European welfare programs and US workers' compensation programs (see cites in North, Wallis and Weingast, 2009: 144).

racies increase investment, encourage economic reforms, improve the provision of schooling and health care and reduce social unrest.

A hurdle to measuring whether democracy contributes to growth is differences in electoral rules, which affect how well elections hold politicians accountable. For example, winner-takes-all versus proportional representation; voting for party lists versus individuals; or run offs versus first past-the-post (candidate with the most votes wins), all have different effects on party control, politicians' incentives, and voter mobilization (for cites and details, see Cox, 2005). We can see this in Box 6.1 on Argentina, which also shows possible negative effects of federalism, our next topic.

6.3.2   Federalism

There is much debate about the benefits of federalism – greater accountability, easier citizen participation, more transparency – versus drawbacks – capture by local oligarchs, a race to the bottom, regional inequity in federal transfers, and so on (Bardhan, 2016). New institutionalists have focused on the specific institutional arrangements (such as rules for revenue and power sharing) under which federalism curbs excessive centralization of power and holds governments accountable. Weingast (1995; 2005; 2007) suggests that "market preserving federalism" can arise if subnational jurisdictions compete to foster local prosperity and those that abuse their power and fail to encourage markets risk losing capital and labor to other localities. Weingast's conditions for market preserving federalism, however, are demanding: (1) subnational governments need the authority to adjust their policies; (2) products and factors must be mobile across jurisdictions; (3) subnational governments must be prohibited from spending beyond their means; and (4) rules must keep the federal government from unilaterally intervening in subnational affairs. "Many federal systems restrict the policy authority and independence of subnational governments compromising the benefits of federalism. Examples include Mexico throughout much of the late twentieth century; India from independence through the mid-1990s; and Russia under Putin" (Weingast, 2007: 7). Some argue that China is another example (see Section 6.5).

Federalism, like democracy, cannot simply be installed in a society through constitutional engineering. While much research has considered the effects of federalism, more study is needed on the specific circumstances under which market preserving federations are built and sustained. Simison and Ziblatt (2018: 31) argue that understanding federalism, like the study of institutions more generally, requires moving away from formalistic studies of its operation towards greater appreciation of the social conditions that make institutions more or less viable in different contexts.

Federalism may check government through vertical decentralization; next we examine how horizontal decentralization and executive constraints may also curb arbitrary action.

6.3.3 Executive constraints and separation of powers

Constraints on executive power are prominent in NIE explanations of the origins of modern states and how states make credible commitments. One way to constrain executives is to empower other branches of government – legislatures and courts. In this regard, considerable research contrasts three systems (see Alston et al., 2018: 175–9 for cites): (1) presidential systems, such as Brazil or the US, with an executive and one or two legislative chambers elected directly by voters for fixed terms; (2) hybrid systems, such as Bolivia or Poland, with one executive elected by voters and a second chosen by the legislature; and, (3) parliamentary systems, such as Germany or the UK, with a single executive chosen by the legislature who can be dismissed through a vote of no confidence. Superficially, presidential and hybrid systems have more veto gates[9] and thus greater separation of powers than parliamentary systems. However, the literature shows the difficulty of analyzing complex institutions based on such broad distinctions, which cannot fully account for differences in context and history (Alston et al., 2018). Initial studies found substantial difference in outcomes between the three systems, but as institutional details were added and studies spread beyond the US and Europe, these distinctions faded (Carey, 2005). Presidential, hybrid and parliamentary systems have also tended to converge, as legislatures have intervened to remove presidents during times of crises. Furthermore, a legislature only acts as an effective break on the executive if it represents divergent interests, while diverse interests can also constrain executives even without separation of powers if they are important in the ruling coalition (Haggard and McCubbins, 2001). Finally, executives are constrained by

---

[9]   Discussed in Chapter 7: 7.3.

forces that are hard to measure, for example, the threat of electoral defeat or informal institutions such as the norms of political compromise that develop among politicians who repeatedly interact and care about their reputations (Moe and Caldwell, 1994: 180).

Separation of powers, federalism, elections, political parties and civic organizations form part of a configuration of institutions working together to prevent abuse of power and hold state actors accountable. Another powerful component of that configuration is the legal system, which is also crucial to protection of property and human rights and contractual enforcement.

6.4   The NIE approach to legal systems

NIE has continuously focused on the institutional arrangements that allow credible commitments between buyers and sellers and governments and the governed. In that regard, the characteristics of the institutions that provide third-party enforcement of disputes are key. North, Wallis and Weingast (2009: 156) stress the rise of impersonal and impartial laws that are not framed in terms of living individuals, such as kings or bishops, but in terms of abstract and impersonal actors, such as presidents or citizens. In contrast, personal law varies with the individual's status. For example, under Salic law killing a lord resulted in a much bigger penalty than killing a slave (North, Wallis and Weingast, 2009: 155). Impersonal rule of law includes moving from enforcing contracts based on persons to enforcing contracts based on property or *in rem*. This is important because "only in rem rights enable truly impersonal trade to the point that parties can allow themselves the luxury of being totally ignorant of each other's personal attributes, greatly expanding their opportunities for trade and specialization" (Arruñada, 2012b: 2).

Hadfield (2005) points out that equal treatment is not achieved if the legal system is inaccessible or poorly managed. She summarizes the features that make a legal system effective in supporting contractual commitments: (1) low cost, accessible and reliable courts; (2) honest and knowledgeable judges that accurately and faithfully apply the legal rules the parties relied upon when making their contracts; and (3) trained and expert lawyers adhering to professional codes of conduct under judicial oversight, available at reasonable cost. Additionally, the norms of judicial reasoning and the web of procedural rules, property laws, economic regulations, and so on as well as the nature of the contract law itself affect the transaction costs of enforcement. As Hadfield notes, institutional research on these important features is still in its infancy.

Unlike democracy, rule of law consistently has large and significant effects on growth and investment in cross-country regressions, although it is not always clear which specific legal institutions make a difference. Steven (2018: 75) characterizes these variables[10] as measuring "reliability of enforcement of legal rights in general," not just property rights. Some studies measure specific legal institutions and relate them to growth and other variables, although more research is needed. For example, de facto judicial independence is significantly correlated with real GDP per capita in cross-country regressions (Feld and Voigt, 2003; Voigt, Gutmann and Field, 2015). And Voigt (2008) finds independence balanced with judicial accountability reduces corruption (among other things) and explains differences in cross-country income. Alston et al. (2018) also emphasize judicial independence balanced by accountability. Additionally, some studies find that the origins of the legal system have large effects, although this is much debated (Box 6.2).

Box 6.2   The common law versus civil law debate

Does common law perform better than civil law in supporting market exchanges? Common law combines laws passed by legislatures with customary rules and judicial precedents. It gives more discretion to judges, and scholars describe it as more decentralized and bottom-up than civil law (see Rubin, 2005). Common law developed in England to protect private property against the king's encroachment; former British colonies also have common law origins.

Civil law is rooted in Roman law. French civil law was a product of the

---

[10]   These regressions commonly use Freedom House, which asks 26 survey questions about equal treatment under the law, independence of the judiciary, due process, protection from the illegitimate use of force and freedom from war (Freedom House, 2020). Another measure is the International Country Risk Guide (used by Knack and Keefer, 1995) which assesses the risk of expropriation.

Revolution's backlash against a legal system subservient to the king and nobility (Arruñada and Andonova, 2005). Civil law requires judges to uphold laws received from the legislature and comply with the jurisprudence created by higher courts. Countries classified as having civil law origins include France, Italy, Spain, and Portugal and their former colonies as well as Japan and Turkey.

La Porta et al. (1997; 1998; 1999; 2000) argue that civil law, especially French civil law, provides weaker protection of property rights, has fewer checks on state coercion, and is less adaptable to changing circumstances than common law. They find that French civil law origin is statistically correlated with more government intervention, greater bureaucratic inefficiency and less democracy than common law. Beck and Levine (2005) find that common law origins have a positive association with financial development, while Beck, Demirguc-Kunt and Levine (2003) suggest that French civil law origins have a negative association with a measure of protection of property rights.

A number of scholars, however, have challenged the premise that a country's legal origin from decades ago determines how well it protects property rights today (see, e.g., Arruñada and Andonova, 2005; Hadfield, 2005; Shirley, 2008). Others note large differences among countries with the same legal origins (Siems, 2006) and some convergence of common and civil law legal systems (Shirley, 2008). Moreover, since both common and civil law were adopted to prevent the monarchy from encroaching on private property rights and to protect citizens against royal arbitrariness, their differing degrees of judicial discretion may be optimal adaptations to particular circumstances (Arruñada and Andonova, 2005: 246). Berkowitz, Pistor and Richard (2003) provide evidence that the functioning of laws transplanted to colonies depends more upon how well the transplanted laws are adapted to local conditions than on their legal family.

Despite differences, NIE scholars generally regard an effective legal system as a prerequisite for a well-functioning market economy. Yet some countries, such as China, have developed thriving markets without well-established rule of law.

6.5 Countries with weak rule of law or state accountability: the case of China

As we have seen, NIE assumes that a strong state constrained by rule of law and accountable to an informed and organized civil society is a prerequisite for sustainable growth. Yet some countries, notably China since 1978, have grown rapidly without strong formal institutions to prevent abuse of power or protect property rights. Acemoglu and Robinson (2019) observe that property rights in China are not secure, despite a 2007 law providing some guarantees, because courts are not independent and rights heavily depend on political favors. Many scholars argue that a number of informal institutions (described below) have allowed China to develop rapidly despite the weakness of formal safeguards such as rule of law. They contend that these informal institutions supported rapid growth thanks in part to China's favorable conditions[11] including: (1) a long history of strong state capacity and able bureaucracies at the central and local levels that continued with the Communist Party's selection of capable local officials (Xu, 2011; Yao and Zhang, 2015); (2) "regionally decentralized authoritarianism" (Xu, 2011; 2015) where control over personnel, ideology, and politics is centralized in the central government and the Chinese Communist Party (CCP), while administrative functions and economic governance are highly decentralized to provincial governors, mayors and other heads of subnational governments; (3) high degrees of competition among diverse localities for investors and among local officials for promotion; and (4) policies (at least until 2012) promoting factor mobility and other marketization reforms (Zhang, 2019), as well as decentralization of SOE control (Huang et al., 2017) and widespread privatization[12] (Huang et al., 2020) as part of efforts by local officials to improve performance.

Under these supportive conditions, informal institutions protected property and enforced contracts well enough to permit the rapid growth of a vibrant private sector. One such institution was the set of informal norms surrounding the *strong relationship between local government*

---

[11]   Additionally, Zhang (2019) also observes that China started from a low base and had a latecomer's advantage, benefitting from 300 years of technological advances in Western economies.

[12]   Huang et al. (2020) finds the privatization program in China was the largest in the world by revenue and led to major increases in productivity.

officials and businesses. Zhang (2018) notes that many private firms were originally SOEs or township and village enterprises that maintained close ties to local governments. Later, local government officials became stakeholders in (connected) private firms (Cull et al., 2015). Additionally, firms spend lavishly on entertaining local officials (Cai, Fang and Xu, 2011). They also provide them with "special deals" that give them "high powered incentives" to lend a "helping hand" (Bai, Hsieh and Song, 2019). Park and Luo (2001: 455) suggest that local governments and firms have become partners in "an intricate and pervasive relational network that contains implicit mutual obligations, assurances, and understanding" that the Chinese call "guanxi." Guanxi helps protect property rights and enforce contracts in government-to-business as well as business-to-business relations. Although many of these practices are illegal and have resulted in local monopolies, Bai, Hsieh and Song (2019) argue that strong competition between provinces to attract business has limited their predatory power (somewhat similar to Weingast's market supporting federalism).

Also important are *familial and social networks* and *industrial clusters* (Long and Zhang, 2011; Long, 2018), which use trust and cooperation within groups to mediate conflicts and protect property and contracting rights. Nee and Opper (2012; see also Peng and Heath, 1996) argue that China's growth relied on networks, formed by a broad-based, bottom-up movement of private entrepreneurs sharing strong social norms. The movement started below the government's radar in the poorest regions (such the Yangzi delta) and expanded to the point where the private sector became the largest source of jobs, viewed by local authorities as indispensable to economic growth (Nee and Opper, 2012: 228). Furthermore, local governments became increasingly dependent on revenues from private firms and relied on their dynamism to meet their performance targets, especially as SOEs became unable to compete and remained a fiscal drain (Nee and Opper, 2012: 230–1). Greif and Tabellini (2017) also stress kinship networks, documenting the reemergence of clans after government suppression ended with the reforms of the post Mao era.

Such informal institutions do not work for everyone, since by definition networks exclude non-members and smaller firms are less able to court local officials. Farmers in particular have few protections. After fiscal reform centralized tax revenues in the central government in 1994, subnational authorities confiscated land from farmers (who have rights to use land but not ownership) with compensation substantially below market values in order to sell it to developers to meet local revenue needs (Xu, 2011).

Some scholars have a dim view of China's future without more formal institutions such as rule of law. Long (2018) and Xu (2011; 2015) suggest that China's informal substitutes for rule of law are showing strains and contradictions, including unproductive investments, increased corruption and rising unrest from dispossessed farmers. Zhang (2018) further argues that the recentralization of power and the anti-corruption campaign have weakened the incentives of local officials. Similarly, Bai, Hsieh and Song (2019) note that the unfettered ability of local governments to favor certain businesses has waned, leaving in place powerful interests that oppose reform. Both Long and Xu question whether China can meet the demands of an increasingly sophisticated economic and social system without rule of law. Acemoglu and Robinson (2019) argue that a despotic state is unlikely to tolerate the large-scale experimentation and innovation required to move China beyond growth based on existing technologies. Further, Zhang (2018) projects that without stronger institutional constraints, unrestricted government power may squeeze out the private sector. Coase and Wang (2012) also warn that the weakness of China's market for ideas stifles creativity, despite being the largest producer of PhDs in the world. However, some analyses find considerable advances towards rule of law and innovation. For example, Chen et al. (2017) present survey results suggesting rule of law is increasing in China, especially in product markets, and Wei, Xie and Zhang (2017) argue that there is considerable innovation occurring in China, although both papers call for major structural changes.

6.6 Mysteries, puzzles, and new frontiers

This chapter has focused on NIE's treatment of modern states providing broad-based public goods and supporting vibrant markets and prosperous societies, while constrained from arbitrary action by rule of law and civil society. Such institutions are one of humanity's great inventions, yet most people are still governed by far less beneficial structures and a great deal of aid and effort has largely failed to improve them. Despite the extensive literature analyzing Western-style political and legal systems, the question of how to make them effective elsewhere has not been answered (see Chapter 8). Moreover, countries like China that have produced dramatic improvements in prosperity without strong "prerequisite" institutions suggest that the role and limits of informal alternatives demands further study (Long, 2018 suggests research topics on rule of law in China). Moreover, the authors who studied the origins of open access institutions and rule of law did not view them as inevitable or irreversible, and current threats have raised questions about their sustainability.

Besides these broad research questions, there are a number of more specific puzzles, for example, the role of norms – their determinants, consequences, and changes (Voigt, 2018 suggests some topics) – as well as political parties, elections, and collective action (see Keefer, 2018). The continuing debate about the origins of effective states also suggests openings for study. Additional research is also needed to understand more fully how political markets shape not only public policy but also the structures of government, and to understand and measure democracy. Finally, we already highlighted open questions in federalism (for more, see Simison and Ziblatt, 2018) and legal systems (Hadfield, 2015). These are only a few of the many research questions stimulated by institutional analyses of state and legal systems.

PART III

Transversal topics

7 Institutions and public policy

New institutionalists, like most economists and political scientists, view policymaking not as a response by a benevolent government to natural monopoly or externality, but as the outcome of a web of interactions between citizens, policy makers, and policy implementers. While many scholars have focused on the choice of policies, such as optimal levels of taxation, new institutionalists emphasize the structures and processes that determine how policies are decided and implemented, such as rules for legislative decision-making or delegating to tax authorities.

New institutional economics (NIE) contributions to our knowledge of how interest group demands are translated into policy are twofold. First, they explain how different institutional environments – for example, strong democracies governed by impersonal and effective rule of law or weak/non-democracies dominated by powerful elites – affect political behavior, helping unfetter a literature that had previously concentrated on Western democracies. Second, NIE shifted emphasis from median voter, rent seeking, and capture theories to collective action and political bargaining under conditions of information asymmetries, uncertainties, and opportunism.

We begin this chapter with collective action since it determines how citizens' expectations affect politics and policy (7.1). Next, we consider how NIE illuminates our understanding of the ways in which institutional frameworks shape political bargaining in mature democracies and in weak or non-democracies (7.2), and how political bargains affect governance structures and policy design and implementation (7.3), as well as the delegation of powers to public agencies (7.4). We then illustrate the NIE approach by examining the regulation of utilities (7.5). While much progress has been made on these subjects, there are still many challenges for future research (7.6).

7.1 Collective action

To understand public policy, we must first understand the role of the public itself in the formulation of policy. More specifically, how can individuals overcome the collective action hurdles that prevent them from acting together to have a voice in policy? The idea that individuals will not necessarily act in the collective interest was famously articulated by Mancur Olson (1965: 2): "[U]nless the number of individuals in a group is quite small, or unless there is coercion or some other special device to make individuals act in their common interest, rational, self-interested individuals will not act to achieve their common or group interests." A large number of economic experiments and empirical research (see Box 7.1), however, finds that even without coercion or inducement, an important proportion of individuals *are* willing to spend substantial resources to cooperate with strangers to achieve a public good, and are also willing to take costly actions to sanction those who fail to cooperate under certain circumstances (see, e.g., Fehr and Gächter, 2000; Ostrom, 2000; Bowles and Gintis, 2011). Today, "Free riding is now recognized as only one among many possible outcomes of a collective endeavor, so the question is no longer if strategically rational individuals can coordinate at all (they can), but what makes coordination happen, how it is sustained, and what variables affect it" (Medina, 2013: 260). New institutionalists explicitly address the questions posed by Medina.

Box 7.1 What experimental games tell us about collective action

Ostrom (2000) argues that Olson's (1965) assumption that rational, self-interested individuals will not cooperate without inducements may work well in predicting behavior in competitive markets and auctions, but not in all collective action situations. She describes public goods games: economic experiments where all players receive an initial endowment of, for example, $10, and are asked to contribute between $0 and $10 to a common pool – the public good. The contributions are multiplied by a factor, for example 1.5, and then distributed back to all players equally. Thus, if everyone in a group of 10 contributes $10, all the players would receive $15. If nine contribute $10 and one contributes $0, nine would get $13.50 and the free rider would end up with $23.50 (initial endowment of $10 plus $13.50 from the common pool). Olson's assumptions predict that rational, self-interested subjects should contribute $0, under the expectation that they will benefit from the others' contributions and retain their endowment. Ostrom, however, cites the "huge" number of experiments where people contribute between 40 and 60 percent of their endowment in one shot or the first round of repeated games, although cooperation decays over subsequent rounds to almost zero. Cooperation is higher and more sustained if players are allowed to communicate (Ostrom, 2000). Moreover, allowing subjects to punish free riders, even at a cost to the punisher and where much of the benefits go to others, greatly increases cooperation, which stabilizes to about 75 percent of the subjects' endowments (Fehr and Gächter, 2000; Fehr and Schmidt, 2001). However, experiments across countries (Herrmann, Thöni and Gächter, 2008) suggest that rates of punishment vary widely and, in some cases, *high* contributors are also punished.

Keefer (2018: 10) summarizes four preconditions for collective action: (1) convergence of interest; (2) clarity about the distribution of costs and benefits; (3) limits on the extent to which individuals can free ride on the efforts of others; and (4) sufficient communication among members to allow them to act collectively. Early on, Ostrom (1990) drew on extensive field research to describe the institutions that allow communities to manage common pool resources without over-exploitation (detailed in Chapter 3: 3.4). New institutionalists (Greif, 2005; 2006; North, Wallis and Weingast, 2009; Acemoglu and Robinson, 2012; 2019) have also explored how cooperation emerged in the origins of modern state and legal systems (see Chapter 6: 6.2).

The NIE literature suggests that the ability of individuals to act collectively to affect policy depends upon the institutional environment, since it determines the extent to which access is open to entry by new interest groups rather than dominated by a few powerful groups to the exclusion of others. Regardless of the institutional environment, some interest groups may be purely rent seeking, trying to capture policy benefits and special privileges as described by Buchanan, Tollison and Tullock (1980). However, North, Wallis and Weingast (2009) and Acemoglu and Robinson (2019) argue that where access is open, many countervailing interest groups will be able to form to preserve open access by resisting incumbent groups from using their organizational advantage to extract excessive rents (see Chapter 6: 6.3 for more on this). Access is determined by society's basic institutional framework and we turn to that next.

7.2 Political bargains under different institutional environments

7.2.1 The role of political bargains

For NIE, the design, implementation, and sustainability of policies are determined through political bargaining (North, 1990b; Dixit, 1996). As we noted in Chapter 2, political bargains are similar to but also significantly different from economic bargains (see Moe, 1990; also Caballero and Arias, 2013; Caballero and Soto-Oñate, 2016). In economic bargains, the actors and their interests are better defined and more stable. In contrast, the parties to political bargains are often multiple and not always easily identified and the outcome is sensitive to the influence voters and interest groups have over their representatives who make these bargains. As Moe (1990: 227) notes, political bargaining is inherently more uncertain than bargaining within or between firms, because it is a struggle over a temporary control of public authority (and related budgets) that can be abruptly overturned in the next election. Winners can pursue their own interests at the expensive of losers, negating past bargains and imposing new constraints on the way the game will be played in the future. Caballero and Arias (2013: 18–19) and Caballero and Soto-Oñate (2016: 338–9) summarize other reasons given in the literature for high political transaction costs including information problems stemming from the opaque nature of political bargains and the lack of clear measures of results (no equivalent to prices), the absence of enforcement mechanisms, and the short-term horizons of political actors versus the long-run nature of political decisions. Politicians are thus motivated to design structures and norms to reduce uncertainty, promote compromise and narrow the scope for discretion (McCubbins, Noll and Weingast, 1987; 1989; Moe, 1990; Moe and Caldwell, 1994). Such institutional choices are "part and parcel of the policy-making process" (Moe, 1990: 230).

The NIE literature describing political bargaining grew out of positive political theory, which rejected earlier normative theories assuming that government would always act in the public interest to correct market failures. It differs from the Medium Voter Theorem (Downs, 1957; Black,

1958), which assumes that under majority voting politicians will seek to maximize votes by choosing policies close to the preferences of the median voter, and from the so-called Chicago School (Posner, 1969; Stigler, 1971; see also Section 7.4 below), which assumes that policies result from competition among interest groups exchanging votes for redistribution of rents in their favor. It also differs from Public Choice Theory (Buchanan and Tullock, 1962), which assumes self-interested political actors will take advantage of voters' information asymmetries and bargain for policies that work to their political benefit. NIE does not dispute the importance of vote seeking, rent seeking and political self-interest, but unlike these theories, also examines problems of observability and enforcement of legislative bargains over time. Political bargains can be treated as uncertain and incomplete contracts, typically unwritten or even tacit (Caballero and Arias, 2013; Caballero and Soto-Oñate, 2016), subject to opportunism and governed by structures and norms that are purposely designed to lock in policy influence (Moe, 1990; North, 1990b; Dixit, 1996).[1] We consider next how political bargains function under two distinct institutional frameworks: strongly institutionalized democracies and weakly institutionalized and non-democracies.

7.2.2   Political bargains in strongly institutionalized democracies

The early studies of political bargains focused on mature, Western-style democracies (see Chapter 6). North (1990b) and Dixit (1996) described bargains between voters and legislators as tacit, highly uncertain contracts. Shepsle and Weingast (1984; 1987) and Weingast and Marshall (1988) analyzed bargains between US legislators and found that congressional rules of committee structure, seniority, and so on (Box 2.3) were designed to limit their incentives and opportunities to renege, thereby reducing the transaction costs of reaching more credible and durable agreements. Later studies analyzed situations where legislative committees were weak and party leaders were strong (e.g., Spain in Caballero, 2011) or where the executive dominated legislative decisions (e.g., Brazil in Alston and Mueller, 2006).

---

[1]   See Caballero and Soto-Oñate (2016) for a survey of NIE research on political transaction costs and political exchange.

Studies of parliamentary systems (see Carey, 2005 for cites) have revealed such bargaining over policy. Moe (1990) and Moe and Caldwell (1994) suggest that in parliamentary systems, norms of reciprocity and cooptation of interest groups into public agencies facilitate compromise and promote durable bargains. Much of the bargaining over policies in parliamentary systems takes place "within the foundational bargain to form a government" (Carey, 2005: 99).

7.2.3 Political bargains in weak or non-democracies

The literature on weaker democracies and autocracies is more recent. As Gehlbach (2018: 25) asserts, until recently the "overwhelming share of intellectual effort in political economy … was devoted to the study of mature democracies."[2] Yet, most of the world's population lives in, and has always lived in, autocracies or weakly institutionalized democracies. New institutionalists have been increasingly active in exploring these regimes (see, e.g., Levi, 1988; Acemoglu, Robinson and Verdier, 2004; North, Wallis and Weingast, 2009; Gehlbach and Keefer, 2011).

While some studies differentiate between countries solely on the basis of whether elections take place,[3] new institutionalists look beyond elections. North, Wallis and Weingast (2009), for example, describe how, by controlling organizations, elites guard against independent threats to their hegemony. In such states, democratic institutions (elections, legislatures, political parties) are not permitted to challenge the dominant elite's economic powers. For example, even after the end of the hegemony of Mexico's dominant political party (the PRI) in 2000, the stock market has remained a club of entrenched industrial and financial elites and access of non-elites to banking credit is scarce (Díaz-Cayeros, 2013).

For new institutionalists (e.g., Keefer, 2005; North, Wallis and Weingast, 2009; Cruz and Keefer, 2015) policies in *weak democracies* are the outcome of bargaining among dominant elite groups who compete with

---

[2]   An early exception was Bates (1981), who described how dominant elites in Africa manipulated agricultural and foreign exchange policies to keep prices low and win the support of urban elites.

[3]   Consider, for example, Besley and Persson (2019) which relies on the PolityIV database to categorize Mexico, Russia, Sweden, and the UK in one group – countries that have made a permanent switch to democracy.

one another for rents and interact with the rest of the population through extensive patron-client relationships. These relationships are implicit contracts, where patrons provide protection and benefits to their clients who reciprocate by providing rents and services (including votes) to the patron. (In mature democracies clientelism is condemned as corruption, see Box 7.2.) Patron-client relationships are often sustained by machine politics, whereby a clientelist political party builds commitment and selectively buys votes of less committed voters with food, clothing and services as well as cash (Stokes, 2005). Stokes shows that such parties, once important in the US, are common in Latin America, and describes how they embed themselves in the social networks of working-class neighborhoods to persuade and monitor voters.[4]

Box 7.2   What deters political corruption?

Which institutions foster or deter political corruption, defined as the misuse of public office for political gain? The answer to this important question has proved elusive, despite considerable research. Golden and Mahdavi (2015) summarize research that finds that: (1) poor democracies are as likely to be corrupt as poor autocracies; (2) parliamentary systems are more associated with corruption than presidential systems in some models, while in others the reverse holds; (3) different electoral systems (e.g., open versus closed list) determine corruption in some specifications and not in others; (4) federalism is and is not associated with corruption depending on the countries in the data set; and (5) judicial independence reduces corruption in some circumstances and not in others. They also find that cross-country research and subnational research give divergent answers.

Golden and Mahdavi do find one regularity, however: political corruption is robustly and negatively correlated with wealth. Many of today's wealthy countries once suffered the same levels of massive corruption as today's poor countries, but became relatively less corrupt as they developed. However, researchers have not been able to make convincing

---

4   In Argentina, for example, the Peronist Party distributed food and clothing. They also printed and distributed ballots, which increased the likelihood that someone would vote for Peronist candidates from 7 percent to 13 percent (Stokes, 2005).

causal identification of the institutional changes that led rich countries to curb corruption.

"The strong cross-sectional relationship that we observe today – the least corrupt countries are wealthy, whereas the more corrupt are poor and middle income – is merely one result of the poorly understood process by which improvement in government and governance accompany economic development" (Golden, 2018: 171). Research on more fine-grained micro-institutions has proved promising, particularly on the transformation of political parties from patronage machines to programmatic parties that provide voters the information they need to hold politicians accountable for corrupt practices (see Chapter 6: 6.3).

Even in *autocracies* there is evidence of bargaining among the factions in the executive branch. Nobel (2018: 1421) argues that "authoritarian political executives, like their democratic counterparts, contain actors with differing policy preferences." He illustrates how in Russia, unresolved disputes between factions within the executive branch can sometimes lead to squabbles among their proxies in the legislature and to legislative amendments. Lü, Liu and Li (2018) find similar proxy battles over laws related to education in Chinese national assemblies, contrary to their image as purely ceremonial bodies.

Guriev and Treisman (2015) argue that modern autocrats increasingly rely on electoral institutions to manipulate information at a time when the rise in public education and less costly access to global information has reduced the appeal of authoritarian ideologies and made crude and violent repression less effective. By concealing violence and mimicking democracies through elections and legislatures while manipulating the results and repressing opposition candidates, autocrats strive to convince the general public of their competence and emphasize performance in their rhetoric (Guriev and Treisman, 2015).

7.3   Impact of institutions and bargains on policy

The NIE literature has examined various ways that the institutions and bargains we just described affect the nature of policies. One way is through the separation of powers. McCubbins (2005; see also Haggard and McCubbins, 2001) summarizes studies describing how separation of powers gives different political actors or factions the opportunity to block or significantly delay policy, creating so-called veto gates.[5] A veto gate could be the executive branch, the different houses of the legislature, an independent judiciary, even the military in some societies. Polarized veto gates make policies harder to change, hence less flexible but more credible. For example, Keefer and Stasavage (2003) show that monetary policy made by legally independent central banks is more credible in the presence of multiple, polarized veto gates, which increases the scope for the central bank to act independently, reducing inflation and the likelihood of politically motivated turnover of central bank governors.

Polarized veto gates can hinder politicians' efforts to strike intertemporal bargains, especially in societies where governing rules and norms do not support sustainable policies. Spiller and Tommasi (2005) argue that this is the case in Argentina because of institutions (described in Box 6.1) that result in frequent turnover of key actors, high levels of executive discretion, lack of objective third parties (such as an independent bureaucracy or courts), and large short-term payoffs to non-cooperation. Facing such circumstances, politicians sometimes opt for simple, rigid rules, leading to inflexible policies, and sometimes for rules that vary with each political shift, resulting in highly erratic policies that discourage investors (Spiller and Tommasi, 2005: 524–5).

Patron-client contracts also have an effect on policy. Keefer (2005) and Keefer and Vlaicu (2007) argue that elected officials are more likely to rely on such implicit contracts when they cannot credibly commit to voters that they will deliver broad improvements in social policy. In the face of high transaction costs caused by uncertainty and potential opportunism, they and their clients are mainly interested in patronage (jobs, contracts) and policies (private goods) that directly benefit them, with little room for voters to prevent rent seeking. The case studies in North et al. (2013) describe how politicians maintain their power by rewarding patronage and advantage to potential rivals. For example, Zambia under the one-party rule of Kaunda (1972–91) expanded the civil service to the point where it became the largest employer, increased SOEs and expanded price and other controls, all to increase rents available to reward allies (Levy, 2013). In the Philippines under Marcos (1972–86),

---

[5]   Veto gates are a handy way to count the extent of checks and balances.

the sources of rents were different, notably preferential credit allocation and monopoly rights over agricultural markets, but the goal was the same: rewarding cronies to retain their support (Montinola, 2013: 168–71). Creating and allocating rents to maintain elite bargains was essential to the survival of these regimes, which got into trouble when the sources of patronage resources were threatened, for example, by the fall of copper prices in Zambia (Levy, 2013: 123).

7.4   Delegation to public agencies

The same uncertainties and incentives that shape how political actors bargain with each other also affect how they delegate power to public agencies. In a sense, politicians are trying to avoid *ex post* opportunism by bureaucratic agents seeking greater power or autonomy by installing institutions that constrain their freedom of action.[6] McCubbins, Noll and Weingast (1987; 1989) argued in two widely cited papers that a coalition will attempt to design a government agency's administrative procedures to guide its decisions in line with the preferences of the coalition's constituents (for similar studies, see Moe, 2013). Specifically, the dominant coalition will: (1) design procedures that alert politicians and their constituents whenever an agency might be about to change course; (2) impose delays to give them time to intervene before the agency presents them with a fait accompli; and (3) stack the deck in favor of their preferred constituents by, for example, making the agency dependent on those constituents for information.[7] Politicians are motivated to design these *ex ante* institutional constraints because an *ex post*, legislative solution may not be feasible. That could be the case if, for example, rival coalitions in the legislature would support an opportunistic agency. Additionally, *ex*

---

[6]   The large literature on institutions and central bank independence provides empirical evidence for this; see also Weingast and Moran's (1983) study of delegation and the US Federal Trade Commission.

[7]   Epstein and O'Halloran (1999) argue that delegation by the US Congress is akin to a make-or-buy decision. Legislators delegate decisions to the executive when the political benefits are low, preferences are aligned between the politicians and the bureaucrats, and delegated power is relatively simple to monitor (e.g., airline safety). Legislators incur transaction costs to write detailed legislation to reduce agency discretion where these conditions do not prevail so they can privilege valued constituents (e.g., tax policy).

ante constraints may be less costly to legislators than committing time and staff to day-to-day oversight of the agency's decisions.

The institutions that result from political bargaining often purposefully slow action, reduce responsiveness and produce what Williamson (1996: 199) termed "inefficiencies by design." Condemning such inefficiencies "reflects a political disconnect or analytical myopia" since the "inefficiencies that arise by design may not be inefficiencies at all" (Williamson, 1996: 200). The characteristics of public agencies often lead to negative comparisons with private firms, which are seen as less costly and more flexible, but high transaction costs and inflexibility are inherent in the nature of political bargaining and may be the price of compromise and ensuring that original purposes are not quickly reversed. In an extension of Gibbons's (1999; 2005) comparison of markets and firms, Dixit (2012) argues that government agencies are better than markets or firms at coping with the complexities that arise from irreconcilable, conflicting, multiple goals and severe information asymmetries.

This does not mean that reforms to improve efficiency are impossible. Rather, reforms should meet Williamson's "remediableness" condition – feasible alternatives that can be described and implemented with expected net gains. The experience with SOEs illustrates the futility of trying to remove politics from public policy. Some SOEs were created to replace public agencies, while others were nationalized private firms or newly created enterprises. All were expected to pursue government goals with the efficiency of private firms. This effort to evade the realities of politics proved fruitless (see Box 7.3).

Box 7.3 State-owned enterprises (SOEs) and politics[8]

State-owned enterprises (SOEs) grew rapidly in market economies after World War II. By 1980, majority-owned, non-financial SOEs averaged 8 percent of GDP in developed countries, 15 percent in developing countries (Musacchio and Lazzarini, 2014), and exceeded 30 percent in Egypt, Nicaragua, and Zambia (Shirley, 1983, S.A. table 1). Despite

---

[8]   This box is based on Shirley (1983); World Bank (1995); Shirley and Walsh (2000).

a wave of privatizations starting with the UK in 1979 and intensifying throughout the 1990s and 2000s, SOEs are still widespread today and make up some of the largest enterprises in the world (IMF, 2020).

SOEs were created for many reasons, but an underlying goal was to escape the inefficiency, corruption or inflexibility of central bureaucracies and harness the incentives and efficiency of the firm to the service of government objectives.[9] The idea that SOEs would somehow escape politics and be insulated from weak governmental norms and rules, however, was largely deemed to have failed by the early 1990s, as research increasingly documented the political use and abuse of SOEs (Donahue, 1989; Kikeri, Nellis and Shirley, 1992; World Bank, 1995). These included using SOEs to: provide lucrative jobs and state banking credit to the politically well connected, divert revenues and bypass budgetary processes for personal or political gain, keep sensitive prices low for political reasons, fund government budgets at the expense of enterprise maintenance and investment, etc. Over the years, governments have sought ways to improve performance by insulating SOEs from politically motivated interventions while increasing transparency and accountability (for a summary of early reforms, see Shirley and Nellis, 1991 and World Bank, 1995; for more recent efforts, see IMF, 2020). Yet the problem of politically motivated or corrupt interventions remains. This should not have been surprising. NIE tells us that government programs cannot escape politics and institutions simply by transferring them from public bureaus to SOEs. NIE aims for considering all the costs and benefits of feasible and realistic alternatives, as Coase (1960) famously advocated.

In weakly institutionalized countries, inefficiencies often go beyond non-responsiveness to include pervasive incompetence or corruption. Spiller and Tommasi (2007: ch. 6) describe how Argentina's civil service, despite the country's high quality human capital, ranks very low in inter-

---

[9]   An important objective was fiscal revenue. Many had been money losing public agencies (e.g., railroads), others were nationalized money-makers (e.g., oil in Mexico or copper mining in Zambia) or created to generate funds (e.g., Korean or Thai tobacco monopolies). Besides revenues, SOEs were expected to meet social objectives, for example, increasing employment, promoting regional development, redistributing income, and to operate presumed natural monopolies, such as water and sewerage systems.

national ratings of competence and in public confidence. They attribute this to Argentina's institutional weaknesses described in Box 6.1.

Under some circumstances, politicians may prefer an incompetent to a competent civil service. Keefer (2018: 17) points out that while politicians want to implement their favored programs, "a well-organized public administration reduces politician discretion and authority over public policy" because civil servants recruited on merit and bound together by an ethic of public service are less susceptible to political influence. A competent and honest civil service is a public good with wide benefits to the public, but narrow and immediate costs to politicians who rely on patronage and to civil servants who benefit from the status quo. More research is needed to understand when politicians are motivated to improve civil service capacity. One important factor is the capacity of citizens to punish politicians who fail to pursue their preferred policies. Cruz and Keefer (2015) find that programmatic political parties, which can help citizens overcome their collective action problems and hold politicians accountable (see Chapter 6, also Box 7.2), play an important role. Similarly, Golden and Mahdavi (2015) cite papers suggesting that political parties may be relevant for control of corruption, calling for more research.

A clear and consequential example of how governments operate in the ways just described is the case of utility regulation, where application of NIE has provided important insights.

7.5   The case of utility regulation

Just as with political markets, NIE's perspective on utility regulation is different. The Chicago School treats rent seeking as the core issue for regulatory design and proposes escaping the risk that self-interested actors capture the regulatory agency by restoring market forces through, for example, privatizing or unbundling so-called natural monopolies. Although NIE contributors acknowledge the real threats of regulatory capture and rent seeking, they focus not on optimal regulation, but on understanding how the specifics of regulation are embedded in their institutional environment and how they adapt (or fail to adapt) to changing circumstances. For example, new institutionalists consider the extent to which separation of powers, judicial independence, electoral and other political rules, and dependence on foreign aid might curb arbitrary actions by governments or regulators. The NIE's perspective also differs from the incentive approach of Laffont and Tirole (1993), which prioritizes the design of optimal contracts and regulators, specifying *ex ante* rules about pricing, subsidies, entry, and so on, to increase efficiency. Although new institutionalists recognize the importance of the design of contracts and the status of regulators, they also emphasize the need for *ex post* adaptability to unexpected events while maintaining the credibility of the contractual bargain (Spiller and Tommasi, 2005; Spiller, 2010). This requires attention to, for example, how easily laws can be changed to overturn contract provisions, whether regulators have the power to compel compliance with the contract, whether utilities have the option to appeal to an independent and impartial judicial system, what are the political advantages and disadvantages of government opportunism, and so on.

As with political bargains, NIE treats utility regulation as a type of long-term, incomplete contract (Goldberg, 1976; Williamson, 1976; Joskow, 1991). Although the specifics vary according to the regulated activity and the broader institutional conditions, in the NIE perspective regulations aim for two main goals: (1) support and secure the rights of investors and (2) deliver efficient (with respect to quality and cost) services to consumers. The NIE literature proposes that the credibility and effectiveness of regulation depend on: (1) the institutions that frame and enforce regulation; (2) the transaction costs of regulation; and (3) the procedures to adapt regulation to unforeseen events while avoiding contractual hazards.

7.5.1 Institutions that frame and enforce regulations

In the NIE perspective, the credibility and effectiveness of regulation depends upon such institutions as constraints on arbitrary executive power, safeguards of the independence and impartiality of judiciaries, rules affecting the quality of the administrative apparatus, even the social norms and ideologies that frame agents' behavior (Levy and Spiller, 1994). Examples of empirical studies of the institutional/regulation interactions include case studies of cable television (CATV, Williamson, 1976), the electric power industry (Joskow, 1989), telecommunications reform (Levy and Spiller, 1996), municipal water reform (Savedoff and Spiller, 1999; Shirley, 2002), and numerous others.[10]

7.5.2   Transaction costs

In considering the transaction costs of regulatory contracts, there is general agreement among new institutionalists (well synthesized in Savedoff and Spiller, 1999; and Spiller, 2010) that utilities are different. Specifically, they combine: (1) economies of scope and scale, approaching monopolistic positions; (2) a high ratio of sunk investments, making the protection of investors a key and politically sensitive issue; (3) a large set of differentiated consumers who also act as political forces; and (4) high risks of opportunistic behavior by all parties involved. This combination challenges the sustainability of utility regulation by, for example, exposing it to political cycles, and threatens its credibility by, for example, exposing it to capture. As a result, the development, monitoring, and enforcement of long-term regulatory contracts (including less formal agreements if the utility is publicly owned) have high transaction costs. For the same reasons, the transaction costs of shifting from one arrangement to another, such as moving from concession contract to reliance on the market or franchise bidding,[11] are also high, as we can see with the difficulties in implementing public-private partnerships, for example. A fundamental lesson from NIE is "the need to examine tradeoffs between alternative organizational and contractual arrangements and to reject the assumption that 'the free market' can always replicate efficiently internal organizations and complex contractual arrangements" (Joskow, 1991: 79; also Joskow and Noll, 2013).

7.5.3   Adapting while circumventing contractual hazards

As we have seen in earlier chapters, a key consideration for new institutionalists is the risk of contractual hazards, especially opportunistic behavior. All parties to utility regulation might act opportunistically: (1) governments by changing the rules of the game arbitrarily; (2) regulators

---

[10]   Several cases of regulation, from classic utilities to the financial sector, are analyzed from the NIE perspective in Menard and Ghertman (2009).

[11]   Opposing views of franchise bidding as a market alternative to regulation can be seen by comparing, for example, Williamson (1976) and Goldberg (1976) with Demsetz (1969) and Posner (1969).

by interpreting and implementing the law; (3) firms, both public and private, by strategically using price discrimination or quality control or by otherwise exploiting information asymmetries; and (4) third parties, such as well-organized interest groups, by challenging or otherwise obstructing decisions. These hazards help explain the reliance on rigid rules to protect against political games and discretionary power at the cost of flexibility, for example, setting a maximum fixed price that utilities can charge (in effect, a price cap) rather than a rate-of-return or other variable rule. In weakly institutionalized democracies or non-democratic regimes, the risk that powerful elites may challenge the monitoring and enforcement of contracts and capture the regulator for their own ends may even make vertical integration a better solution than regulation (Spiller, 2009).

Although a substantial part of NIE literature on regulation has focused on utilities, this contractual framework is also relevant for other areas of public policy (e.g., antitrust, see Joskow, 1991; 2002; or common pool resources, see Libecap, 2008a; 2014).

7.6   Challenges for the future

There has been great progress in demonstrating human capacity for collective action and describing how conditions for fostering cooperation emerged in history and expanded in societies. Our understanding of the workings of the institutions that translate collective action into policy design and implementation has also greatly advanced. Yet many challenges and opportunities remain. For example, the operation of collective action is, in Phil Keefer's words (2018: 9), "still a mystery." Keefer poses a number of research questions which the literature reviewed in this chapter has not fully answered and that can be summarized as: "Under what circumstances do citizens succeed in overcoming the collective action problem of holding governments accountable for social progress?" (Keefer, 2018: 9).

Weak and non-democracies present another area demanding more research, as Gehlbach (2018) reminds us. Even the way we distinguish democracies from dictatorships can be much improved. Objective measures of whether elections are contested and how many parties compete may not tell us if the parties out of power have a reasonable chance of ever winning office (Teorell, 2018). Corruption also presents a wealth of potentially rewarding avenues for research; Golden (2018: 176) lists a number of them.

These are just a sample of the stimulating research topics posed by the NIE approach to public policy.

8 Institutional change and development

Generations of economists have pondered Adam Smith's question – why are some countries rich and others poor? From its inception, the Northian branch of new institutional economics (NIE) has been captivated by this question, prompting an outpouring of research. Initially, this research concentrated on confirming that institutions are a significant determinant of economic development, one that dominates rival explanations (8.1). These studies demonstrated that the effects of institutions were not only significant but also long-lasting. In the search to explain this persistence and why and when institutions change, new institutionalists have concentrated on four themes: powerful elites (8.2); path dependency (8.3); beliefs (8.4); and more recently, culture (8.5). The result is a rich and varied body of research, but there is still much fruitful work to be done to answer Smith's famous question (8.6).

8.1 Institutions as determinants of economic development

Research on development has always been a NIE focus, and over time the emphasis has broadened. Early studies concentrated especially on explanations for the rise of modern, democratic states and impersonal rule of law in Western Europe, as we described in Chapter 6. The scope widened with the transition from communism in Central and Eastern Europe and the former Soviet Union beginning in 1989 (see studies cited in Gehlbach and Malesky, 2012) and growing interest in less developed countries and non-democracies (e.g., de Capitani and North, 1994). Work on diverse systems has expanded ever since, as we can see in Chapter 7.

When NIE began in the early 1970s, explanations for underdevelopment did not usually include institutions. For example, North (1986: 953) asserted "Among economic historians, technological change has always held the pre-eminent position as a source of economic growth." His paper showed that technology alone could not explain productivity improvements in ocean shipping from 1600 to 1850 and it "knocked technology off its throne" (Menard and Shirley, 2014: 19). Easterly (2002) nicely summarizes other prominent explanations for development, notably investment and innovation, sound macro-economic policies, and education. Easterly finds scant evidence that these "engines of growth" actually determine growth in less developed countries. Shirley (2008: 17) summarizes the now widespread view that: "underinvestment, lack of a good education, and bad policies are proximate causes of underdevelopment, but they are not ultimate causes."

The ultimate cause according to North (1990a: 107) are institutions – "the underlying determinant of the long-run performance of economies." He asserted that economic performance depends upon institutions because laws, rules, and norms determine the cost of transacting and producing and hence the incentives to invest, transact, learn, innovate (as explained in Chapter 1). North and subsequent scholars focused on how changes in fundamental institutions (such as constitutions and basic shared norms) affect development. He and other scholars (e.g., North, 1990a; 2005; Greif and Laitin, 2004; Greif, 2006; Aoki, 2007) also argued that continual changes in less foundational institutions (such as regulations, contracts, norms of doing business) prompt changes in the larger institutional framework (see Section 8.3 for more on this).

North's contention that institutions determine long-run growth was not a new idea. Many economists, including Hayek, Schumpeter, and the old institutionalists, all shared this view. North's message, however, was strengthened by pathbreaking empirical studies finding institutions played an important role in US and European history (Davis and North, 1971; North and Thomas, 1973 [1999]; Greif, 1993; 2006) and that they have large and significant correlations with per capita GDP growth and investment in cross-country growth regressions. One early and influential example of the latter was Knack and Keefer (1995), which found that proxies for security of property and contractual rights had large effects on investment and growth.[1] A vast body of subsequent research similarly found that variables measuring institutional quality have consistently

---

[1]   They used ratings from private risk assessment services to develop proxies for risk of expropriation, rule of law, government repudiation of contracts, bureaucratic quality and the like, which have been widely used in subsequent studies.

large and significant correlations with growth and other measures of economic performance (for cites, see Aron, 2000, table 1; Pande and Udry, 2005, table 1; Shirley, 2008, table 5.1; and Durlauf, 2018, table 1). Among the institutions found to be significant for growth in these regressions were measures of protection of property rights, enforcement of contracts, and rule of law; economic freedom (voluntary exchange, free competition, protection of people and property, etc.); civil liberties and democracy; political instability (negatively correlated); and institutions supporting cooperation (trust, religion, social clubs, etc.).[2]

Measuring a complex concept such as an institution at a cross-national level is a challenge. Initial studies used broad abstractions representing composites of institutions (such as rule of law) that were based on surveys of subjective opinions of "experts" in simple OLS regressions. These measures sometimes confused institutions and outcomes (Shirley, 2008) and obscured "important dimensions of heterogeneity" (Pande and Udry, 2005: 31). With time, however, both measures and methodologies have become increasingly sophisticated. Concerns over endogeneity prompted researchers to develop a number of instrumental variables (listed in Durlauf, 2018, table 2). One well-known example was Acemoglu, Johnson and Robinson (2001), which used rates of settler mortality 100 years ago as an instrument. The authors argued that in places where few European colonialists settled because they feared deadly diseases (malaria, yellow fever), the colonial powers imposed extractive institutions that protected only elites' property rights with few checks on government abuse of power. Their regressions showed that such extractive institutions persisted and have a negative impact on institutions (measured as the risk of expropriation) and per capita GDP today.

More recent studies use increasingly refined methodologies and unique new data sets to measure the impact of institutions, frequently focusing on within country variation to reduce endogeneity, missing variables, and unobserved heterogeneity. (For historical studies, see Nunn, 2009; and for within country studies, see Pande and Udry, 2005, table 4.) A good example of this is Dell's study of the effects of the colonial forced labor system in Bolivia and Peru described in Box 8.1.

---

[2]   Shirley (2008: ch. 5) discusses these indicators in detail.

Box 8.1   Institutional persistence: the long-term effects of forced labor in colonial Peru and Bolivia

Dell (2010) analyzes the impact of the *mita*. From 1573 to 1812, the colonial rulers required indigenous communities in a designated *mita* area of present-day Bolivia and Peru to provide one-seventh of their adult male populations to work in gold and silver mines. Using a regression discontinuity approach, Dell was able to analyze almost identical households along the boundary of the *mita*'s jurisdiction. She found that areas once subject to the *mita* have 25 percent lower household consumption today and 6 percent greater prevalence of stunted growth in children.

Strikingly, Dell also explored how the *mita* could affect current living standards almost 200 years after its abolition. In contrast to other studies (notably Engerman and Sokoloff, 1997), she argues that the *absence* of large landholdings (*haciendas*) in the *mita* areas was one channel for the persistent negative *mita* effects. To avoid competition for labor, the Spanish colonial government restricted the formation of *haciendas* in *mita* areas, promoting communal land tenure instead. Dell hypothesizes that *hacienda* owners, who had secure tenure, lobbied for greater provision of public goods, such as roads, in their areas. In contrast, the Peruvian government abolished communal property soon after the *mita* ended without creating an enforceable titling system for peasants, leading to confiscations of peasant lands, rebellions, banditry, and livestock rustling. Today *mita* areas have less educational attainment, greater prevalence of subsistence farming, and are less integrated into road networks.

Not all scholars accept the primacy of institutions. For example, McCloskey (2016b; see also 2006; 2010) argues that radical changes in ideas, ethics, rhetoric, and ideology are much more important to understanding growth and development than "mere" institutional improvements. New institutionalists increasingly incorporate beliefs and what is often termed culture into their analysis (see Sections 8.4 and 8.5), although they usually view them as coevolving or precipitating institutional change. Others (e.g., Gallup, Sachs and Mellinger, 1998; Sachs, 2003), propose geography as the ultimate cause of development because of its effects on agricultural productivity, the prevalence of dangerous diseases, and transport costs.[3] Scholars emphasizing institutions don't deny the importance of geography, but argue that its impact is indirect, through institutions. Thus, Engerman and Sokoloff (1997; 2002) claim that where geography favored large plantation agriculture with enslaved people (e.g., the US South or Latin America), colonists in the new world designed political and legal institutions to preserve their power by limiting access to property, suffrage, education, credit, and so on. Acemoglu, Johnson and Robinson (2001; 2002) also portray geography as operating through institutions: tropical areas harbor insects carrying dangerous diseases and contain land more suitable for plantation agriculture, geography deterred colonial settlement and prompted colonial powers to impose extractive institutions. Rodrik, Subramanian and Trebbi (2004) find little evidence that geography matters for growth once they control for institutions.

While no single study is without flaws, the large numbers of diverse studies led Durlauf (2018: 2) to conclude, "this breadth of evidentiary forms has given credibility to empirical institutional economics, allowing for the emergence of robust evidence of the importance of institutions and robust recommendations for policy." While he cites the "many empirical successes," he also notes "many unanswered questions."

The most fundamental of these questions are: why do societies not choose the institutions that promote growth and development? And when and why do institutions change?[4] NIE contributors addressing these questions usually focus on changes in macro institutions, what North (1990a; 2005) called the institutional framework and Alston et al. (2018) referred to as the fundamental institutions of governance. In this chapter we do not include NIE research that treats this institutional framework as largely exogenous, even while recognizing that changes in day-to-day rules and norms may eventually provoke changes in more fundamental institutions. There are many examples of this research in our previous chapters, such as Libecap, Ostrom, and their followers on how competition among groups changes property rights institutions in Chapter 3 and

---

[3]   Others argue that geography has indirect effects on development through its impact on agriculture and domestication of animals (Diamond, 1997).

[4]   See Kingston and Caballero (2009) for a partial survey of institutional change theories in NIE and OIE.

Williamsonian analyses of changes in governance and organizations in Chapters 4 and 5.

Numerous studies find that macro institutions (e.g., constitutional guarantees and rules, protections of property rights, adherence to impersonal laws, norms of civic activism, etc.) persist over time. The NIE literature provides four answers to the questions of why fundamental macro institutions are hard to change: (1) dominance of economic and political elites; (2) path dependency; (3) beliefs; and, more recently, (4) culture. These explanations lie on a spectrum and most theories combine elements of several or all of them. For ease of exposition, we will consider each separately along with the corresponding explanations for when and why each hurdle is overcome and institutions change.

8.2 How institutions persist and when and why they change: elite dominance

8.2.1 How elite dominance makes institutional change difficult

A large NIE literature (Chapters 6 and 7) describes how elites who benefit from the status quo prevent non-elites from organizing to change it. Acemoglu, Egorov and Sonin (2020: 3) summarize the argument: "groups that are empowered by current institutions benefit from these institutions and thus use their power in order to maintain them, in the process reproducing their own power over the future institutions." North (1981; 1990a) and North, Wallis and Weingast (2009) go even further and suggest that only elites can overcome the barriers to collective action and become the driving force for institutional change. Explanations invoking dominance of "economic and political elites" are widespread (see North, 1990a; Engerman and Sokolof, 1997; North, Wallis and Weingast, 2009; Acemoglu and Robinson, 2012; Alston et al., 2018). Even though the identity of the dominant groups may change, these authors argue that the fundamental institutions tend to persist as a source of economic and political power. For example, Acemoglu, Johnson and Robinson (2001) argue that after colonialism ended, the post-colonial elites exploited the same extractive institutions that had sustained and enriched the colonial powers. Powerful groups also purposely design institutions and pursue policies to solidify their privileged position over the long term (Acemoglu,

Egorov and Sonin, 2020).[5] For example, Acemoglu and Robinson (2006) explain the resistance to industrialization by the Russian and Hapsburg Empires as an attempt to preempt forces that might lead to institutional change.

8.2.2 When and why do institutions change?

A number of NIE authors portray the proximate cause of institutional change as the result of elite power plays, even while recognizing the deep roots of change in prior history and the role of other factors, such as beliefs (Shirley, 2008; North, Wallis and Weingast, 2009; Acemoglu and Robinson, 2012; Alston et al., 2018; Acemoglu, Egorov and Sonin, 2020). For example, Acemoglu, Egorov and Sonin (2020) describe changes when some members of the dominant group prefer a new arrangement, perhaps because flaws in the old arrangements have become apparent and intolerable over time. Examples include Britain's Glorious Revolution (North and Weingast, 1989), and the elite-driven reform movement in the Soviet Union in the 1980s (Acemoglu, Egorov and Sonin, 2020). North, Wallis and Weingast (2009) describe a more gradual process whereby elites find it profitable to transform their personal privileges into impersonal rights and gradually widen access. (Elite-driven changes may be the result of a shock; something we consider in the next section.)

Acemoglu, Egorov and Sonin (2020) note that sometimes the "disempowered majority" overcome their collective action problems and threaten elite control. These non-elites may take power and impose major institutional change (e.g., the Bolshevik Revolution in 1917) or the elites may respond to pressure from below by undertaking institutional reforms to forestall worse outcomes (e.g., extension of suffrage in nineteenth century England).[6] The authors note, however, that in other cases, elites have responded to such pressure by increasing repression; the choice depends partly on history, which we consider next.

---

[5] We saw such persistence by design at the micro-level in Chapter 7.
[6] Reforms intended to prevent rebellion can have the opposite effect, however. Finkel, Gehlbach and Olsen (2015) show that nineteenth century Russia's emancipation of the serfs exacerbated the unrest it was expected to curtail.

8.3 How institutions persist and when and why they change: path dependency

8.3.1 How path dependency makes institutional change difficult

The incentives motivating powerful groups to preserve institutions are linked and reinforced by historical choices and network effects that make it much more economically and politically costly to change the status quo than it was to install it originally. North (1990a: 95–6) described such path dependence as the idea that when a new institution is formed, organizations evolve to take advantage of the new framework, with direct and indirect effects on other organizations, leading to the creation of informal constraints that modify and extend the formal rules, all of which results in an interdependent web that is costly to change.[7] Path dependence is not "a story of inevitability in which the past predicts the future" (North, 1990a: 98); rather it "narrows the choice set and links decision making through time." Greif (2006: 194) argues that "institutional elements inherited from the past are part of the initial conditions of processes that lead to new ones ... new institutions are not created de novo, but emerge or are established by marginally altering elements inherited from the past" (see Box 8.2).

Box 8.2 Path dependency in medieval Genoa and Venice

Greif (2005; 2006) describes how path dependency explains the emergence of superficially similar political organizations with profoundly different implications in late medieval Genoa and Venice. During the eleventh century, the two Italian city states were governed by powerful rival clans. Venice's leader was an elected monarch, the doge, who allocated rents under strict rules that benefitted all clans and did not give any one clan an incentive to try to dominate the others. Venice's

---

[7] The usual example of path dependency is found in technology: the QWERTY keyboard has persisted in the face of more efficient alternatives because of large setup costs, learning effects, coordination effects (advantages to cooperation with other economic agents taking similar action), and adaptive expectations (when prevalence on the market enhances beliefs of further prevalence) (David, 1975; Arthur, 1988 cited in North, 1990a: 93).

system weakened clan identity and fostered norms of loyalty to the city, which flourished. Genoa operated under a non-Genoese *podestá*, who was hired with his military contingent every year to create a military balance of power among the clans. The rival clans continued to build military power, develop patronage networks and strengthen clan identity, and eventually the system collapsed. The choices of the two cities were path dependent. Unlike Venice, Genoa's military power and wealth were highly concentrated and it had a tradition of centralized rule (2005: 758). Moreover, Genoa's norms justified the use of force to achieve political aims, and citizens shared the belief that one clan would challenge another if the appropriate opportunity emerged (2006: 198). Greif concludes that Venice's less concentrated social structure, more widespread distribution of wealth and power, tradition of a coordinating rule rather than a system of mutual deterrence, and different norms and shared beliefs led to its different institutional development.

8.3.2 When and why do institutions change?

Despite path dependency, institutions do change, which new institutionalists explain as the product of: (1) an endogenous process of accumulation of marginal changes, or (2) an exogenous shock. In the first explanation, the continual marginal changes in the day-to-day rules of the game that occur in response to competition between organizations, entrepreneurs, or interest groups eventually lead to deeper changes in more fundamental institutions (North, 1990a; 2005; Greif and Laitin, 2004; Greif, 2006; Aoki, 2007).[8] For example, in the case of Genoa in Box 8.2, the cooperation between clans increased their wealth but also their temptation to try to capture it. The clans' continual investment in increasing their military ability to attack other clans and fortifying their residences, expanding their networks, and indoctrinating clan members in norms of revenge, eventually undermined the *podestá*, the institution they had created to secure clan cooperation (Greif and Leitin, 2004: 643).

---

[8]   DellaPosta, Nee and Opper (2017) describe how such change may happen from the bottom up. Random deviations from an otherwise stable institutional equilibrium may allow sufficient returns to reward the initial actor and also to attract others to imitate deviant behavior. Network effects may spread the behavior so widely that state authorities feel compelled to accommodate the new behavior. They illustrate this with the rise of private manufacturing in Wenzhou and Shanghai since 1978.

In other studies, a shock or discontinuity sometimes propels institutional change despite path dependency. Williamson (2000: 598) points to rare windows of opportunity created by civil wars (Britain's Glorious Revolution), occupations (Japan and Germany after World War II), perceived threats (Japan's Meiji Revolution), breakdowns (former Soviet Union), military coups (Chile) or financial crises (New Zealand). Acemoglu and Robinson (2012: 432) also discuss shocks that lead to "critical junctures" ("historical turning points"). Whether critical junctures lead to fundamental institutional change is still contingent upon earlier history, however. For example, in the mid-fourteenth century, peasants in Western Europe had gradually gained more power and autonomy than in Eastern Europe, and as a result of this disproportionate power, when the Black Death reduced the workforce in Europe it led to the dissolution of feudalism in the West but only contributed to a "Second Serfdom" in the East (110).

Historical limitations are sometimes forcefully overcome through mass revolution. Vahabi, Batifoulier and Da Silva (2020) describe how during the French Revolution of 1789, the peasant and urban poor united with the bourgeoisie behind a negative agenda of destroying the old institutions. Despite the subsequent turmoil, the rise of a military dictatorship under Napoleon and the restoration, the Revolution still partly destroyed an important part of France's aristocratic privileges and feudal institutions. A number of institutional innovations resulted, including the civil law code, equality before the law, the secularization of the state, state administration based on merit rather than economic power, and many more (Vahabi, Batifoulier and Da Silva, 2020: 883–4).

8.4 How institutions persist and when and why they change: beliefs

8.4.1 How beliefs make institutional change difficult

In the NIE literature, shared societal beliefs lead people (sometimes mistakenly) to view their institutional arrangements as superior and resist change. For scholars who view institutions as rules, beliefs are integral to explanations for elite dominance and path dependency. For example, North (2005: 2) asserts that the "dominant beliefs" of those powerful enough to make policy motivate the "accretion of an elaborate structure of institutions" that imposes "severe constraints" on those seeking to modify existing institutions. Similarly, Alston et al. (2018: ch. 8) propose a framework in which "dominant beliefs" must change for institutions to change. Beliefs in these studies are accumulated over time, shared across society, and embodied in informal institutions such as norms and conventions (North, 2005).

Beliefs are even more crucial for those who view institutions as an equilibrium in games with multiple equilibria (e.g., Greif and Laitin, 2004; Myerson, 2004; Greif, 2006; Aoki, 2007). Thus, Aoki (2007: 6) asserts that "agents' shared beliefs about how the game is played and to be played" makes institutions "self-sustaining patterns of social interaction." In other words, every member of society shares the same beliefs about what is the "right thing to do" under a given circumstance and they share the same expectations that others will conform to the rules and that others expect them to conform to the rules and punish non-conformers; as a result, beliefs generate the regularity in behavior that equates to an institution. As Greif (2006: 158–9) puts it: "The observed behavior reproduces the beliefs that generated it, because it confirms each individual belief that others will behave in a particular manner, and given these beliefs, it is optimal for each individual to do so." Similarly, Greif and Mokyr (2017: 26) argue that a society's beliefs and experience are distilled into its shared "cognitive rules," which are the basis for "institutions – rules, expectations, and norms."

8.4.2 When and why do institutions change?

In the NIE explanation, beliefs change enough to allow institutions to change when there is an anomaly between expectations and outcomes. For Aoki, Greif, and Greif and Laitin, who view institutions as equilibria, a cumulative buildup of behaviors or circumstances destabilizes shared behavioral beliefs and eventually upsets the equilibrium, leading to endogenous institutional change. For those who view institutions as rules, sufficiently large divergences between beliefs and outcomes produce an opportunity for change. For example, Alston et al. (2018, part III) point to large deviations between outcomes and expectations in the US after the 1776 revolution when the former colonies were still weak and divided. They argue that leaders with legitimacy and entrepreneurship (e.g., George Washington and Alexander Hamilton) can change the dominant elite's shared beliefs about governance (e.g., opposition to a strong alliance between the states), bringing about a "critical transition," when fundamental institutions change (e.g., the signing of the Constitution in 1786 and the transition from states' rule to the United States). Similarly, Shirley (2008: ch. 7) suggests that shocks or threats to powerful elites whose past reform efforts have failed, increased their willingness to consider a viable alternative supported by a role model. She emphasizes the role of local experts seen by elites as knowledgeable, truthful, and disinterested, who persuade those in power to effect change. The experts also help promulgate the new paradigm among interest groups whose beliefs need to change for the new institutions to be sustainable. She gives the example of Taiwan, where Kuomintang leaders who had escaped from mainland China after the Revolution faced the shock of China's rising growth and international presence in the 1980s, combined with pressure to yield more power to native Taiwanese. These circumstances made them receptive to a group of influential economists advocating for institutional reform.

8.5   How institutions persist and when and why they change: culture

8.5.1   How culture makes institutional change difficult

The final reason in the NIE literature for why people may not choose more adequate institutions is "culture": people embedded in shared cultures derive utility from the status quo above and beyond the economic benefits or costs. In economics, culture has various meanings. Empirical studies typically follow Guiso, Sapienza and Zingales (2006) in defining culture as beliefs and values transmitted fairly unchanged from generation to generation. In many studies, the definition also includes norms and conventions, in which case culture includes North's informal institutions.

The resurgence of culture as an explanation for institutional persistence is partly the result of important research by anthropologists, including field experiments (see Ensminger and Henrich, 2014; Henrich, 2016; 2020) that find very different behaviors in economic experiments across cultures, and research suggesting that humans are a culturally evolved species (Box 8.3).[9]

Box 8.3   An anthropological explanation of how culture affects institutions[10]

Anthropologist Joseph Henrich surveys a large body of research showing that culture is a consequence of adaptations that led humans to rely on learning from other people. Early humans who learned to imitate role models developed skills, tools, and behaviors that enabled them to survive better as a group than as individuals (2016: 192). As humans increasingly interacted in ever larger groups and with outsiders, their social norms became partially internalized, to the point where people automatically comply with local norms without conscious reflection (2016: 189). Such culturally transmitted social norms eventually clustered into initially informal and then formal institutions (2020: 68), such as marriage rules that regulate who individuals can marry, how many spouses they can have, etc. The agglomeration of people into larger groups and the Christian Church's marriage and family rules that reduced the power of kinship ties, among other forces, gradually contributed to societies where members are more individualistic, less conformist, less distrustful of strangers, more cooperative in new groups with strangers, more responsive to third-party punishment, and more personally honest (as opposed to honest only within kinship groups), traits evidenced in economic experiments and in other behavior, such as donating blood (Henrich, 2020: 226–7).

The result was what Henrich terms "market norms" which "establish the standards for judging oneself and others in impersonal transactions and lead to the internalization of motivations for trust, fairness, and cooperation with strangers and anonymous others" (2020: 293). These norms contribute to a culture in which people are far more cooperative with anonymous other players in public good games than people from

---

[9]   Similarly, Bowles and Gintis (2011) argue that institutions are the result of a cultural transmission process based on learned behaviors.

[10]   Based on Henrich (2016; 2020). He defines culture as "the large body of practices, techniques, heuristics, tools, motivations, values, and beliefs that we all acquire while growing up, mostly by learning from other people" (2016: 2).

isolated, small-scale hunter-gather or farming communities (see cites in Henrich, 2020; also Ensminger and Henrich, 2014).

Although recent, this literature is too large to do justice to it here (for a survey, see Alesina and Guiliano, 2015). Among the cultural traits most researched as important to economic development according to Alesina and Giuliano (2015) are those which lead to trust (see Box 8.4) or generally honest behavior (Tabellini, 2007) towards people outside one's kinship group. Additionally, studies have investigated the effects of more individualistic cultures, those that put greater emphasis on individual accomplishments and freedom, versus more collectivistic cultures, those putting greater emphasis on group cooperation. For example, Greif (1994) contrasts how Genoa's individualistic culture prompted them to create formal institutions such as law courts rather than rely solely on social networks, while the collectivist cultural beliefs of eleventh century Maghribi traders led them to rely on group institutions to share information and punish deviant behavior within their network.

It has proven difficult to distinguish culture from formal institutions in empirical studies. The two "interact and evolve in a complementary way, with mutual feedback effects. Thus, the same institutions may function differently in different cultures, but culture may evolve in differing ways depending on the type of institutions" (Alesina and Giuliano, 2015: 938). Mueller (2018) argues that culture and institutions coevolve, whereby cultural beliefs guide the choice of institutions. We can see some of these issues in the literature on trust (Box 8.4). Some studies have tried to sort out the interaction between culture and institutions by surveying second generation immigrants' views of such issues as woman's labor force participation or labor market regulation (for a survey, see Fernández, 2010). These studies suggest that some cultural traits "travel with people when they move to a society with different institutions and values" (Alesina and Giuliano, 2015: 904), and persist, perhaps over generations.

Box 8.4   Trust

Trust is the most studied social trait according to Alesina and Giuliano (2015). This literature relies heavily on surveys asking: "generally speaking, would you say that most people can be trusted or that you can't be too careful when dealing with others?" This "generalized trust" in strangers has a large and statistically significant relationship to economic development. Some hypothesize that trust reduces transaction costs by lessening costly spending on security and protection (see, e.g., Knack and Keefer, 1997; Zak and Knack, 2001). However, Levi (2000: 139) points out that the generalized trust measured in these surveys is a "belief, not a behavior" which is difficult to understand without "adequate knowledge of the institutional arrangements or the professional norms that delimit action" since these influence expectations that the trusted will not harm the trustor. And indeed, Zak and Knack (2001) find that trust is higher in countries with strong institutional safeguards for enforcing contracts and reducing corruption (as well as in countries with less income or land inequality or where ethnic heterogeneity has increased exposure to and trust in non-group members). Williamson (1993: 486) described this as "institutionalized trust," noting that "transactions are always organized (governed) with reference to the institutional context (environment) of which they are a part." Institutional safeguards against exploitation allow agents to make credible commitments and engage in informed risk taking with less need for "transaction specific supports" (Williamson, 1993: 476).[11]

Williamson's institutional safeguards, however, require trust that those enforcing the safeguards will not abuse their position. This is illustrated by Keefer et al.'s (2019) study of 90 self-governing food markets in Lima, Peru. The markets that grew the fastest, and were most resilient in the face of the entry of supermarkets were those with the best formal institutions. Specifically, they had an elected board that enforced the rules, invested in market infrastructure, provided collective services (e.g., cleaning), and collected dues. These were also the markets where the founding vendors all came from the same slum neighborhood where they had formed strong informal ties. Thus, research to measure trust as distinct from institutions faces problems of feedbacks and overlaps similar to those that bedevil broader research assessing the

---

[11]   Williamson argued that trust is irrelevant to commercial exchange because "opportunistic agents will not self-enforce open-ended promises to behave responsibly" (1993: 469). In his view, generalized trust is no substitute for credible commitment. However, he did allow (476–7) that "cultures that condone lying and hypocrisy" have fewer societal checks on opportunism, creating contractual hazards that lead them to rely on more generic transactions (such as spot markets).

relationship between formal institutions and culture.

8.5.2 When and why do institutions change?

The difficulties in identifying culture as a variable distinct from institutions has hampered research on when cultures might permit institutional change. Indeed, in some formulations it seems impossible. For example, Williamson (2000) characterized culture, along with informal institutions, traditions, norms, and religion, as "embedded," changing only over centuries or millennia.

However, a number of scholars do not accept that informal institutions necessarily change so slowly. For example, Mackie (1996) shows that foot binding in China was sustained for a thousand years by a self-enforcing convention, but changed in a generation once that convention was disrupted. Other studies have shown relatively rapid changes in attitudes towards women working, premarital sex, and working on Sundays in the US, and towards the role of the state in East versus West Germany (see Gershman, 2017 for a survey). Fernández (2013) provides a possible explanation for why cultures change sometimes slowly and other times quickly. She models changes in cultural beliefs about married women working outside the home in the US as a rational, intergenerational process of learning. As more and more women work, the private and public signals about payoffs get stronger – and when wages go up, the informativeness of the signals increase – and beliefs rationally evolve. The model does a good job in explaining the sometimes slow and sometimes rapid changes in the participation of women in the US labor force over the last 120 years. The literature on how culture is transmitted and changes and its effects on institutional change is growing rapidly, but there are still many puzzles.

8.6 Answering Adam Smith's question

While new institutionalists have made progress explaining the transition to modern state and legal systems in Western Europe, they have been less successful in understanding why demonstrably poorly performing institutions prevail in so many countries despite reform efforts. Extensive research has demonstrated that institutions matter in cross-country growth regressions, and by unbundling institutions, we are beginning to comprehend how economic and political or formal and informal institutions interact and affect outcomes, but there is still much to be done. An explosion in computing power, digitized data, and new methodologies creates exciting opportunities for breakthroughs in analyzing institutions with due regard for their complexity and heterogeneity (Prüfer and Prüfer, 2018).

One of the most stimulating and challenging areas for future work on development is norms and culture. Voigt (2018: 148) describes such "internal" institutions as one of "the major unknowns in institutional economics." He calls for more reliable measures and research on their role and determinants, what happens when formal and informal institutions are in conflict, and when and how informal institutions change. More work is also needed to understand why some values and informal institutions sometimes change quickly and other times slowly (following Fernández, 2013). Mueller (2018: 159) calls for more research to understand the complex interaction between culture and institutions, a line of inquiry that is "wide open for researchers capable of finding untapped cases where a focus on culture and institutions can be shown to improve our understanding." Such understanding requires a "wide lens informed by history, economics sociology, and anthropology – the comparative strength of the New Institutional Economics" and "a match made in heaven" according to Fernández (2018: 194).

Finally, perhaps because a major success of NIE was to refocus economic research from technology to institutions as a driver of productivity and growth, NIE has evidenced a bias towards neglect of the role of technology (Menard, 2014: 581). A better understanding of the complex interactions between technology and institutional change is a priority for future research.

We have just touched on a few of the many rich opportunities to explore why and when institutions change and how this affects development, pointing the way to a strong and rewarding research agenda.

9 Entering new terrains: the future of NIE

This book briefly summarized the central tenets and principal contributions in new institutional economics (NIE) and its vigorous, diverse, and ambitious research agenda. NIE's future portends exciting new inquiries, many of which we have mentioned in earlier chapters and detailed in our companion book (Menard and Shirley, 2018). We expect that future NIE research will expand on its solid base and also address less studied areas such as, rules and norms within firms; the role of technology in institutional and organizational change; the nature and change of informal institutions (norms, conventions, habits); and the relationship between institutions and values, beliefs, and ideas.

As part of their effort to make their case for institutions, new institutionalists have contributed a treasure trove of data. For example, early on a group at the World Bank developed an online database of political institutions (Beck et al., 2001) that now covers 180 countries for 40 years. Additionally, new institutionalists have long been searching for ways to improve existing institutional measures (Teorell, 2018). They have also contributed a wealth of qualitative data through case studies and surveys that are increasingly suitable to more systematic treatment (Skarbek, 2020). More recently, NIE scholars are exploiting data science techniques, such as data and text mining and machine learning, to digitize the sort of detailed observations required for in-depth institutional analysis (Prüfer and Prüfer, 2018).

NIE's trademark combination of powerful analytical tools with this dogged search for data will produce new insights and allow continued progress towards fulfilling Ronald Coase's prediction that all of economics will become transformed by the themes and tools introduced in what is still widely called "new institutional economics." This is not to suggest that NIE is without critics (see, e.g., Glaeser et al., 2004; Hodgson, 2014; McCloskey, 2016b), some quite harsh; these debates are important, and we regret that they were unfortunately beyond the space of this brief introduction.

As we emphasized at the outset, NIE is not a single theory, but a tree with a strong conceptual trunk. Throughout this book we have specified the concepts, the "golden triangle," that bind NIE's branches to one another. Despite these shared ideas, NIE is not a monolithic theory, as we cautioned at the outset. Besides housing a diversity of approaches, there are also many divergent views, even over fundamentals (e.g., between North and Greif over the definition of institutions or Allen and others over the definition of transaction costs). Space did not permit us to explore all the controversies and debates, and we encourage interested readers to probe further. The relatively extensive references listed at the end of this book provide initial guidance in that respect.

Finally, a strength of NIE that goes beyond the brief indications provided in this book is its policy relevance. Early on, founders of NIE analyzed issues with major policy implications, for example, transaction cost considerations in regulation of social costs (Coase, 1960) or monopolies and oligopolies (Williamson, 1975: chs 11 and 12), the implications of institutional economics for development aid (de Capitani and North, 1994), and policies towards communal governance of common pool resources (Ostrom, 1990). NIE's origins in the study of real-world phenomena and empirical testing help explain its appeal to policy makers and practitioners, as well as to scholars and officials from developing countries where the effects of transaction costs and market and institutional failures are especially immediate and widespread and neoclassical equilibria seem especially remote.

It has been the purpose of this short book to summarize the fundamental insights already provided by NIE and to give indications about the rich domains that remain to be explored. The future of NIE is now in the hands of the new generation of researchers in economics and social sciences that have learned the central lessons from its founders and initial contributors: institutions are at the core of our understanding of how societies and economies work.

Bibliography

Acemoglu, D. and S. Johnson (2005), 'Unbundling institutions', *Journal of Political Economy*, **113** (5): 949–95.

Acemoglu, D. and J.A. Robinson (2006), *Economic Origins of Dictatorship and Democracy*, Cambridge: Cambridge University Press.

Acemoglu, D. and J.A. Robinson (2012), *Why Nations Fail: The Origins of Power, Prosperity, and Poverty*, New York: Crown.

Acemoglu, D. and J.A. Robinson (2016), 'Paths to inclusive political institutions', in J. Eloranta, E. Golson, A. Markevich, and N. Wolf, eds., *Economic History of Warfare and State Formation*, Berlin: Springer: 3–50.

Acemoglu, D. and J.A. Robinson (2019), *The Narrow Corridor. States, Societies, and the Fate of Liberty*, New York: Penguin Press.

Acemoglu, D., S. Johnson, and J.A. Robinson (2001), 'The colonial origins of comparative development: an empirical investigation', *American Economic Review*, **91** (5): 1369–401.

Acemoglu, D., S. Johnson, and J.A. Robinson (2002), 'Reversal of fortune: geography and institutions in the making of the modern world income distribution', *Quarterly Journal of Economics*, **117** (4): 1231–94.

Acemoglu, D., J.A. Robinson, and T. Verdier (2004), 'Kleptocracy and divide and rule: a model of personal rule', *Journal of the European Economic Association, Papers and Proceedings*, 2: 162–92.

Acemoglu, D., S. Johnson, and J.A. Robinson (2005), 'Institutions as a fundamental cause of long-run growth', in P. Aghion and S.N. Durlauf, eds., *Handbook of Economic Growth*, Vol. 1a, Oxford and Amsterdam: Elsevier: 386–464.

Acemoglu, D., S. Naidu, P. Restrepo, and J.A. Robinson (2015), 'Democracy, redistribution and inequality', in A. Atkison and F. Bourguignon, eds., *Handbook of Income Distribution*, Vol. 2b, Oxford and Amsterdam: Elsevier: 1885–966.

Acemoglu, D., S. Naidu, P. Restrepo, and J.A. Robinson (2019), 'Democracy does cause growth', *Journal of Political Economy*, **27** (1): 47–100.

Acemoglu, D., G. Egorov, and K. Sonin (2020), 'Institutional change and institutional persistence', NBER Working paper No. 27482, accessed on December 1, 2020 at http://www.nber.org/papers/w27852.

Alchian, A.A. (1965), 'Some economics of property rights', *Il Politico*, **30** (4): 816–29.

Alchian, A.A. (1993), 'Property rights', in *The Concise Encyclopedia of Economics,* accessed on April 1, 2020 at https://www.econlib.org/library/Enc/PropertyRights.html.

Alchian, A.A. and H. Demsetz (1972), 'Production, information costs and economic organization', *American Economic Review*, **62** (5): 777–95.

Alchian, A.A. and H. Demsetz (1973), 'The property rights paradigm', *The Journal of Economic History*, **33** (1), The Tasks of Economic History: 16–27.

Alchian, A.A. and S. Woodward (1987), 'Reflections on the theory of the firm', *Journal of Institutional and Theoretical Economics*, **143** (1): 110–37.

Alchian, A.A. and S. Woodward (1988), 'The firm is dead. Long live the firm', *Journal of Economic Literature*, **26** (1): 65–79.

Alesina, A. and P. Giuliano (2015), 'Culture and institutions', *Journal of Economic Literature*, **53** (4): 898–944.

Allen, D.W. (1991), 'What are transaction costs?', *Research in Law and Economics*, **14** (Fall): 1–18.

Allen, D.W. (2000), 'Transaction costs', in B. Bouckaert and G. De Geest, eds., *Encyclopedia of Law and Economics, Volume 1. The History and Methodology of Law and Economics*, Cheltenham, UK and Northampton, MA, USA: Edward Elgar: 893–926.

Allen, D.W. (2012), *The Institutional Revolution. Measurement and the Economic Emergence of the Modern World*, Chicago, IL: University of Chicago Press.

Allen, D.W. and D. Lueck (2003), *The Nature of the Farm: Contracts, Risk, and Organization in Agriculture*, Cambridge, MA: MIT Press.

Alston, E., L.J. Alston, B. Mueller, and T. Nonnenmacher (2018), *Institutional and Organizational Economics. Concepts and Applications*, Cambridge: Cambridge University Press.

Alston, L.J. and R. Higgs (1982), 'Contractual mix in Southern agriculture since the Civil War: facts, hypotheses and tests', *Journal of Economic History*, **72** (2): 327–53.

Alston, L.J. and B. Mueller (2006), 'Pork for policy: executive and legislative exchange in Brazil', *Journal of Law, Economics, and Organization*, **22** (1): 87–114.

Alston, L.J., G.D. Libecap, and B. Mueller (1999), *Titles, Conflict, and Land Use: The Development of Property Rights and Land Reform on the Brazilian Amazon Frontier*, Ann Arbor, MI: University of Michigan Press.

Anderson, E. and H. Gatignon (2005), 'Firms and the creation of new markets', in C. Menard and M.M. Shirley, eds., *Handbook of New Institutional Economics*, Dordrecht: Springer: 401–34.

Anderson, E. and D. Schmittlein (1984), 'Integration of the sales force: an empirical examination', *Rand Journal of Economics*, **15** (3): 385–95.

Anderson, T.L. and P.J. Hill (2004), *The Not So Wild, Wild West: Property Rights on the Frontier*, Stanford, CA: Stanford University Press.

Aoki, M. (1990), 'Toward an economic model of the Japanese firm', *Journal of Economic Literature*, **28** (1): 1–27.

Aoki, M. (2001), *Towards a Comparative Institutional Analysis*, Cambridge, MA: MIT Press.

Aoki, M. (2007), 'Endogenizing institutions and institutional changes', *Journal of Institutional Economics*, **3** (1): 1–31.

Araral, E. (2013), 'Ostrom, Hardin and the Commons: a critical appreciation and a revisionist view', Singapore: Lee Kwan Yew School of Public Policy Accepted Paper Series No. LKYSPP13-15 (October 10, 2013).

Argyres, N. and K. Mayer (2007), 'Contract design as a firm capability: an integration of learning and transaction cost perspectives', *The Academy of Management Review*, **32** (4): 1060–77.

Argyres, N., J. Bercovitz, and K. Mayer (2007), 'Complementarity and evolution of contractual provisions: an empirical study of IT services contracts', *Organization Science*, **18**: 3–19.

Argyres, N., J. Bercovitz, and G. Zanarone (2019), 'The role of relationship scope in sustaining relational contracts between firms', *Strategic Management Journal*, **41** (2): 222–45.

Aron, J. (2000), 'Growth and institutions: a review of the evidence', *World Bank Research Observer*, **15** (1): 465–90.

Arrow, K.J. (1969), 'The organization of economic activity: issues pertinent to the choice of market versus non-market allocation', in *The Analysis and Evaluation of Public Expenditure. The PPB System*. US Joint Economic Committee, Vol. 1, Washington, DC: US Government Printing Office: 47–64.

Arrow, K.J. (1974), *The Limits of Organization*, New York: Norton.

Arruñada, B. (2003) 'Property enforcement as organized consent', *Journal of Law, Economics, and Organization*, **19** (2): 401–44.

Arruñada, B. (2012a), 'Property as an economic concept: reconciling legal and economic conceptions of property rights in a Coasean framework', *International Review of Economics*, **59** (2): 121–44.

Arruñada, B. (2012b), *Institutional Foundations of Impersonal Exchange: The Theory and Policy of Contractual Registries*, Chicago, IL: University of Chicago Press.

Arruñada, B. and V. Andonova (2005), 'Legal institutions and financial development', in C. Menard and M.M. Shirley, eds., *Handbook of New Institutional Economics*, Dordrecht: Springer: 229–50.

Arthur, W.B. (1988), 'Self-reinforcing mechanisms in economics', in P.W. Anderson, K.J. Arrow, and D. Pines, eds., *The Economy as an Evolving Complex System*, Reading, MA: Addison-Wesley: 9–32.

Azariadis, C. (1975), 'Implicit contracts and underemployment equilibria', *Journal of Political Economy*, **83**: 1183–202.

Bai, C-E., C-T Hsieh, and Z.M. Song (2019), 'Special deals with Chinese characteristics', NBER Working Paper No. 25839, accessed on March 19, 2021 at http://www.nber.org/papers/w25839.

Baker, G., R. Gibbons, and K. Murphy (1994), 'Subjective performance measures in optimal incentive contracts', *Quarterly Journal of Economics*, **109** (4): 1125–56.

Baker, G., R. Gibbons, and K. Murphy (1999), 'Informal authority in organizations', *Journal of Law, Economics and Organization*, **15**: 56–73.

Baker, G., R. Gibbons, and K. Murphy (2002), 'Relational contracts and the theory of the firm', *Quarterly Journal of Economics*, **117** (1): 39–84.

Baker, G., R. Gibbons, and K. Murphy (2008), 'Strategic alliances: bridges between "Islands of Conscious Power"', *Journal of the Japanese and International Economies*, **22** (2): 146–63.

Bardhan, P. (2016), 'State and development: the need for a reappraisal of the current literature', *Journal of Economic Literature*, **54** (3): 862–92.

Barnard, C.I. (1938), *The Functions of the Executive*. Cambridge, MA: Harvard University Press.

Barzel, Y. (1977), 'Some fallacies in the interpretation of information cost', *The Journal of Law and Economics*, **20** (2): 291–307.

Barzel, Y. (1982), 'Measurement costs and the organization of markets', *Journal of Law and Economics*, **25** (2): 27–48.

Barzel, Y. (1989, reprinted 1997), *Economic Analysis of Property Rights*, Cambridge: Cambridge University Press.

Barzel, Y. (2000), 'The state and the diversity of third-party enforcers', in C. Menard, ed., *Institutions, Contracts and Organizations. Perspective from New Institutional Economics*, Cheltenham, UK and Northampton, MA, USA: Edward Elgar: 211–33.

Barzel, Y. (2015), 'What are "property rights", and why do they matter? A comment on Hodgson's article', *Journal of Institutional Economics*, **11** (4): 719–23.

Barzel, Y. and L.A. Kochin (1992), 'Ronald Coase on the nature of social cost as a key to the problem of the firm', *Scandinavian Journal of Economics*, **94** (1): 19–31.

Bates, R.H. (1981), *Markets and States in Tropical Africa: The Political Basis of Agricultural Policies*, Los Angeles, CA: UCLA Press.

Bates, R.H., A. Greif, M. Levi, J-L Rosenthal, and B.R. Weingast (1998), *Analytic Narratives*, Princeton, NJ: Princeton University Press.

Beck, T. and R. Levine (2005), 'Legal institutions and financial development', in C. Menard and M.M. Shirley, eds., *Handbook of New Institutional Economics*, Dordrecht: Springer: 251–78.

Beck, T., G.R.G. Clarke, A. Groff, P. Keefer, and P.P. Walsh (2001), 'New tools in comparative political economy: the database of political institutions', *World Bank Economic Review*, **15** (1): 165–76.

Beck, T., A. Demirguc-Kunt, and R. Levine (2003), 'Law, endowments and finance', *Journal of Financial Economics*, **70** (2): 137–81.

Ben-Porath, Y. (1980), 'The F-connection: families, friends, and firms and the organization of exchange', *Population and Development Review*, **6** (March): 1–30.

Bénabou, R. and J. Tirole (2003), 'Intrinsic and extrinsic motivation', *Review of Economics Studies*, **70** (3): 489–520.

Benham, L. (2005), 'Licit and illicit responses to regulation', in C. Menard and M.M. Shirley, eds., *Handbook of New Institutional Economics*, Dordrecht: Springer: 591–608.

Berkowitz, D., K. Pistor, and J.F. Richard (2003), 'Economic development, legality, and the transplant effect', *European Economic Review*, **47** (1): 165–95.

Berle, A.A., Jr and G.C. Means (1932), *The Modern Corporation and Private Property*, New York: MacMillan.

Bernstein, L.E. (1992), 'Opting out of the legal system: extralegal contractual relations in the diamond industry', *Journal of Legal Studies*, **29** (January): 115–59.

Bernstein, L.E. (2015), 'Beyond relational contracts: social capital and network governance in procurement contracts', *Journal of Legal Analysis*, **7** (2): 561–621.

Bernstein, L.E. (2019), 'Contract governance in small world networks: the case of the Maghribi traders', *Northwestern University Law Review*, **113** (5): 1009–70.

Besley, T. and T. Persson (2019), 'Democratic values and institutions', *American Economic Review: Insights*, **1** (1): 59–76.

Black, D. (1958), *The Theory of Committees and Elections*, Cambridge: Cambridge University Press.

Bowles, S. and H. Gintis (2011), *A Cooperative Species: Human Reciprocity and Its Evolution*, Princeton, NJ: Princeton University Press.

Boyd, R. and P.J. Richerson (1985), *Culture and the Evolutionary Process*, Chicago, IL: University of Chicago Press.

Bradach, J. (1997), 'Using the plural form in the management of restaurant chains', *Administrative Science Quarterly*, **42** (2): 276–303.

Bradach, J. and R. Eccles (1989), 'Price, authority, and trust: from ideal types to plural forms', in R. Scott, ed., *Annual Review of Sociology*, **15**: 97–118.

Brinton, M. and V. Nee, eds. (1998), *The New Institutionalism in Sociology*, New York: Russell Sage Foundation.

Buchanan, J.M. (1975), 'A contractarian paradigm for applying economic theory', *American Economic Review*, **65** (May): 225–30.

Buchanan, J.M. (1985), *Liberty, Markets, and State: Political Economy in the 1980s*, New York: New York University Press.

Buchanan, J.M. and G. Tullock (1962), *The Calculus of Consent: Logical Foundations of Constitutional Democracy*, Ann Arbor, MI: University of Michigan Press.

Buchanan, J.M., R.D. Tollison, and G. Tullock, eds. (1980), *Towards a Theory of the Rent Seeking Society*, College Station, TX: Texas A&M University Press.

Butler, M.R. and R.F. Garnett (2003), 'Teaching the Coase theorem: are we getting it right?', *American Economic Review*, **31** (2, June): 133–45.

Caballero, G. (2011), 'Institutional foundations, committee system and amateur legislators in the governance of the Spanish congress: an institutional comparative perspective (USA, Argentina, Spain)', in N. Schofield and G. Caballero, eds., *Political Economy of Institutions, Democracy and Voting*, New York: Springer: 157–84.

Caballero, G. and X.C. Arias (2013), 'Transaction cost politics in the map of the new institutionalism', in N. Schofield, G. Caballero, and D. Kselman, eds., *Advances in Political Economy: Institutions, Modelling and Empirical Analysis*, New York: Springer: 3–31.

Caballero, G. and D. Soto-Oñate (2016), 'Why transaction costs are so relevant in political governance? A new institutional survey', *Brazilian Journal of Political Economy*, **36** (2): 330–52.

Cai, H., H. Fang, and L.C. Xu (2011), 'Eat, drink, firms and government: an investigation of corruption from entertainment and travel costs of Chinese firms', *Journal of Law and Economics*, **54** (1): 55–78.

Carey, J.M. (2005), 'Presidential versus parliamentary government', in C. Menard and M.M. Shirley, eds., *Handbook of New Institutional Economics*, Dordrecht: Springer: 91–122.

Carson, S.J., A. Madhok, and T. Wu (2006), 'Uncertainty, opportunism, and governance: the effects of volatility and ambiguity on formal and relational contracts', *Academy of Management Journal*, **40**: 1058–77.

Chandler, A.D. (1966), *Strategy and Structures*, Boston, MA: MIT Press.

Chandler, A.D. (1977), *The Visible Hand*, Cambridge, MA: Harvard University Press.

Chen, D., S. Deakin, M.M. Siems, and B. Wang (2017), 'Law, trust and institutional change in China: evidence from qualitative fieldwork', University of Cambridge Faculty of Law Legal Studies Research Paper Series No. 15/2017, accessed July 21, 2020 at https://ssrn.com/abstract=2898174.

Cheung, S.N.S. (1969a), *A Theory of Share Tenancy*, Chicago, IL: University of Chicago Press.

Cheung, S.N.S. (1969b), 'Transaction costs, risk aversion and the choice of contractual arrangements', *Journal of Law and Economics*, **12**: 23–45.

Cheung, S.N.S. (1983), 'The contractual nature of the firm', *Journal of Law and Economics*, **26** (April): 1–21.

Cheung, S.N.S. (1989), 'Economic organization and transaction costs', in J. Eatwell, M. Milgate, and P. Newman, eds., *Allocation, Information and Markets. The New Palgrave*, London: Palgrave Macmillan: 77–82.

Ciliberto, F., G.C. Moschini, and E.D. Perry (2017), 'Valuing product innovation: genetically engineered varieties in U.S. corn and soybeans', Center for Agricultural and Rural Development, Iowa State University Working Paper 17-WP-576.

Coase, R.H. (1937), 'The nature of the firm', *Economica*, **2** (1): 386–405.

Coase, R.H. (1947), 'The origin of the monopoly of broadcasting in Great Britain', *Economica*, **14** (55): 189–210.

Coase, R.H. (1959), 'The Federal Communications Commission', *Journal of Law and Economics*, **2** (October): 1–40.

Coase, R.H. (1960), 'The problem of social cost', *Journal of Law and Economics*, **3**: 1–44.

Coase, R.H. (1972, reprinted 1988), 'Industrial organization: a proposal for research', in *The Firm, The Market, and the Law*, Chicago, IL: University of Chicago Press: 57–74.

Coase, R.H. (1984), 'The new institutional economics', *Journal of Institutional and Theoretical Economics*, **140** (1984): 229–31.

Coase, R.H. (1988a), *The Firm, the Market, and the Law*, Chicago, IL: University of Chicago Press.

Coase, R.H. (1988b), 'Notes on the problem of social cost', in R.H. Coase, ed., *The Firm, the Market, and the Law*, Chicago, IL: University of Chicago Press: 157–85.

Coase, R.H. (1991, reprinted 2005), 'The institutional structure of production', Nobel Prize Lecture, in C. Menard and M.M. Shirley eds., *Handbook of New Institutional Economics*, Dordrecht: Springer, 31–9.

Coase, R.H. (1998), 'The new institutional economics', *American Economic Review*, **88** (2, May): 72–4.

Coase, R.H. (2000), 'The acquisition of Fisher Body by General Motors', *Journal of Law and Economics*, **43** (1): 15–32.

Coase, R. and N. Wang (2012), *How China Became Capitalist*, New York: Palgrave Macmillan.

Commons, J.R. (1934), *Institutional Economics*, Madison, WI: University of Wisconsin Press.

Cox, G.W. (2005), 'Electoral institutions and political competition: coordination, persuasion and mobilization', in C. Menard and M.M. Shirley, eds., *Handbook of New Institutional Economics*, Dordrecht: Springer, 69–89.

Cox, G.W. and M.D. McCubbins (2001), 'The institutional determinants of economic policy outcomes', in S. Haggard and M.D. McCubbins, eds., *Presidents, Parliaments, and Policy*, New York: Cambridge University Press: 21–64.

Cox, M., G. Arnold, and S. Villamayor-Tomás (2010), 'A review of design principles for community-based natural resource management', *Ecology and Society*, **15** (4), art. 38.

Crawford, S.E.S. and E. Ostrom (1995), 'A grammar of institutions', *The American Political Science Review*, **89** (3): 582–600.

Crocker, K.J. and S. Masten (1985), 'Efficient adaptation in long-term contracts: take-or-pay provisions for natural gas', *American Economic Review*, **75** (December): 1083–93.

Crocker, K.J. and S.E. Masten (1988), 'Mitigating contractual hazards: unilateral options and contract length', *Rand Journal of Economics*, 19: 327–43.

Crocker, K.J. and K.J. Reynolds (1993), 'The efficiency of incomplete contracts: an empirical analysis of Air Force engine procurement,' *RAND Journal of Economics*, **24** (1): 126–46.

Cruz, C. and P. Keefer (2015), 'Political parties, clientelism, and bureaucratic reform', Inter-American Development Bank Working Paper 6968, accessed on July 10, 2020 at https://ideas.repec.org/p/idb/brikps/6968.html.

Cull, R., W. Li, B. Sun, and L.C. Xu (2015), 'Government connections and financial constraints: evidence from a large representative sample of Chinese firms', *Journal of Corporate Finance*, **32** (1), 271–94.

Dahlman, C.J. (1979), 'The problem of externality', *Journal of Law and Economics*, **22** (1): 141–62.

David, P. (1975), 'CLIO and the economics of QUERTY', *American Economic Review*, **75**: 332–7.

Davis, L.E. and D.C. North (1971), *Institutional Change and American Economic Growth*, Cambridge: Cambridge University Press.

De Capitani, A. and D.C. North (1994), 'Institutional development in Third World countries: the role of the World Bank', World Bank: HRO Working Paper No. 13685.

De Long, B.J. and A. Shleifer (1993), 'Princes and merchants: European city growth before the industrial revolution', *Journal of Law and Economics*, **36** (2): 671–702.

Dell, M. (2010), 'The persistent effects of Peru's mining *mita*', *Econometrica*, **78** (6): 1863–903.

DellaPosta, D., V. Nee, and S. Opper (2017), 'Endogenous dynamics of institutional change', *Rationality and Society*, **29** (1): 5–48.

Demsetz, H. (1967), 'Towards a theory of property rights', *American Economic Review*, **57** (2): 347–59.

Demsetz, H. (1969), 'Information and efficiency: another viewpoint', *Journal of Law and Economics*, **12** (1): 1–22.

Dewees, C.M. (1998), 'Effects of individual quota systems on New Zealand and British Columbia fisheries', *Ecological Applications*, **8** (1) Supplement: S133–38.

Diamond, J. (1997), *Guns, Germs and Steel: The Fate of Human Societies*, New York: Norton & Co.

Díaz-Cayeros, A. (2013), 'Entrenched insiders: limited access order in Mexico', in D.C. North, J.J. Wallis, S.B. Webb, and B.R. Weingast, eds., *In the Shadow of Violence. Politics, Economics, and the Problems of Development*, Cambridge: Cambridge University Press: 233–60.

Dixit, A.K. (1996), *The Making of Economic Policy: A Transaction Cost Perspective*, Cambridge, MA and London: MIT Press.

Dixit, A.K. (2012), 'Bureaucracy, its reform, and development', *Review of Market Integration*, **4** (2): 135–57.

Donahue, J.D. (1989), *The Privatization Decision: Public Ends and Private Means*, New York: Basic Books.

Downs, A. (1957), *An Economic Theory of Democracy*, New York: Harper and Row.

Durlauf, S.N. (2018), 'Institutions, development and growth: where does the evidence stand?', Economic Development and Institutions Working Paper No. WPI8/04I.

Easterly, W. (2002), *The Elusive Quest for Growth. Economists' Adventures and Misadventures in the Tropics*, Cambridge, MA: MIT Press.

Edwards, D.M. and E. Pinkerton (2019), 'Priced out of ownership: quota leasing impacts on the financial performance of owner-operators', The University of British Columbia Working Paper Series No. 2019-03, accessed on June 14, 2020 at http://fisheries.sites.olt.ubc.ca/files/2019/06/Working-Paper-2019-03 -Priced-Out.pdf.

Eggertsson, T. (1990), *Economic Behavior and Institutions*, Cambridge: Cambridge University Press.

Eggertsson, T. (2015), 'Demand for wealth reducing institutional change: the role of ideas and interests', in N. Schofield and G. Caballero, eds., *The Political Economy of Governance. Institutions, Political Performance and Elections*, Cham, Switzerland: Springer: 3–20.

Engerman, S.L. and K.L. Sokolof (1997), 'Factor endowments, institutions, and differential growth paths among new world economies', in S. Haber, ed., *How Latin America Fell Behind*, Stanford, CA: Stanford University Press: 260–304.

Engerman, S.L. and K.L. Sokolof (2002), 'Factor endowments, inequality, and paths of development among new world economies', *Economia*, **3** (1): 41–88.

Ensminger, J. (1997), 'Changing property rights: reconciling formal and informal rights to land in Africa', in J.N. Drobak and J.V.C. Nye, eds., *The Frontiers of the New Institutional Economics*, San Diego, CA: Academic Press: 165–96.

Ensminger, J. and J. Henrich, eds. (2014), *Experimenting with Social Norms: Fairness and Punishment in Cross-Cultural Perspective*, New York: The Russell Sage Foundation Press.

Epstein, D. and S. O'Halloran (1999), *Delegating Powers. A Transaction Cost Politics Approach to Policy Making under Separate Powers*, Cambridge: Cambridge University Press.

Fama, E.F. (1980), 'Agency problems and the Theory of the Firm', *Journal of Political Economy*, **88** (1): 288–307.

Fama, E.F. and M.C. Jensen (1983), 'Separation of ownership and control', *Journal of Law and Economics*, **26** (2): 301–25.

Fehr, E. and S. Gächter (2000), 'Cooperation and punishment in public goods experiments', *American Economic Review*, **90** (4): 980–94.

Fehr, E. and K. Schmidt (2001), 'Theories of fairness and reciprocity – evidence and economic applications', University of Zurich, Institute for Empirical Research in Economics, Working Paper No. 75.

Feld, L.P. and S. Voigt (2003), 'Economic growth and judicial independence: cross country evidence using a new set of indicators', *European Journal of Political Economy*, **19** (3): 497–527.

Fernández, R. (2010), 'Does culture matter?', NBER Working Paper No. 16277, accessed on September 15, 2020 at http://www.nber.org/papers/w16277.

Fernández, R. (2013), 'Cultural change as learning: the evolution of female labor force participation over a century', *American Economic Review*, **103** (1): 472–500.

Fernández, R. (2018), 'Family and gender: questions for the new institutional economics', in C. Menard and M.M. Shirley, eds., *A Research Agenda for New Institutional Economics*, Cheltenham, UK and Northampton, MA, USA: Edward Elgar: 189–95.

Finkel, E., S. Gehlbach, and T.D. Olsen (2015), 'Does reform prevent rebellion? Evidence from Russia's emancipation of the serfs', *Comparative Political Studies*, **48** (8): 984–1019.

Fisher, S. (1977), 'Long-term contracting, sticky prices, and monetary policy', *Journal of Monetary Economics*, **3**: 317–24.

Fitzpatrick, D. (2005), '"Best practice" options for the legal recognition of customary tenure', *Development and Change*, **36** (3): 449–75.

Freedom House (2020), 'Freedom in the world 2020 methodology', accessed on June 30, 2020 at https://freedomhouse.org/reports/freedom-world/freedom-world-research-methodology.

Freeland, R.F. (2000), 'Creating hold-up through vertical integration: Fisher Body revisited', *Journal of Law and Economics*, **43** (1): 33–66.

Frey, B. (2001), *Inspiring Economics*, Cheltenham, UK and Northampton, MA, USA: Edward Elgar.

Frey, B. (2017), 'Policy consequences of pay for performance and crowding out', *Journal of Behavioral Economics for Policy*, **1** (1): 55–9.

Furubotn, E.G. and R. Richter (1997), *Institutions and Economic Theory. The Contribution of the New Institutional Economics*, Ann Arbor, MI: University of Michigan Press.

Galiani, S. and E. Schargrodsky (2010), 'Property rights for the poor: effects of land titling', accessed on April 11, 2020 at https://ssrn.com/abstract=1544578.

Gallup, J.L., J.D. Sachs, and A.D. Mellinger (1998), 'Geography and economic development', NBER Working Paper No. 6849.

Garner, B.A. and H.C. Black (2005), *Black's Law Dictionary*, St-Paul, MN: Thompson/West.

Gehlbach, S. (2018), 'What is next for the study of non-democracy?', in C. Menard and M.M. Shirley, eds., *A Research Agenda for New Institutional Economics*, Cheltenham, UK and Northampton, MA, USA: Edward Elgar: 20–6.

Gehlbach, S. and P. Keefer (2011), 'Investment without democracy: ruling-party institutionalization and credible commitment in autocracies', *Journal of Comparative Economics*, **39** (2): 123–39.

Gehlbach, S. and E.J. Malesky (2012), 'The grand experiment that wasn't? New institutional economics and the postcommunist experience', in S. Galiani and I. Sened, eds., *Institutions, Property Rights and Economic Growth: The Legacy of Douglass North*, New York: Cambridge University Press: 223–47.

Gerring, J., P. Bond, W. Barndt, and C. Moreno (2005), 'Democracy and growth: a historical perspective', *World Politics*, 57 (3): 323–64.

Gershman, B. (2017), 'Long-run development and the new cultural economics', in M. Cervelatti and U. Sunde, eds., *Demographic Change and Long-Run Development*, Cambridge, MA: MIT Press: 221–61.

Gibbons, R. (1999), 'Taking Coase seriously', *Administrative Science Quarterly*, 44 (1): 145–57.

Gibbons, R. (2005), 'Four formal(izable) theories of the firm?', *Journal of Economic Behavior and Organization*, 58 (2): 200–45.

Gibbons, R. (2010), 'Transaction-cost economics: past, present, and future', *Scandinavian Journal of Economics*, 112 (2): 263–88.

Gibbons, R. (2020), 'Governance economics', in SIOE, Oliver Williamson's Legacy, June 18, accessed June 19, 2020 at https://www.sioe.org/news/governance-economics.

Gibbons, R. and R. Henderson (2012), 'Relational contracts and organizational capabilities', *Organization Science*, 23 (5): 1350–64.

Gibbons, R. and R. Henderson (2013), 'What do managers do?', in R. Gibbons and J. Roberts, eds., *The Handbook of Organizational Economics*, Princeton, NJ: Princeton University Press: 680–731.

Gibbons, R. and J. Roberts, eds. (2013), *The Handbook of Organizational Economics*, Princeton, NJ: Princeton University Press.

Gibson, E.L. (2013), *Boundary Control. Subnational Authoritarianism in Democratic Countries*, Cambridge: Cambridge University Press.

Gil, R. (2013), 'The interplay between formal and relational contracts: evidence from movies', *Journal of Law, Economics, and Organization*, 29 (3): 681–710.

Gil, R. and G. Zanarone (2017), 'Formal and informal contracting: theory and evidence', *Annual Review of Law and Social Science*, 13: 141–59.

Glaeser, E., R. La Porta, F. Lopez-de-Silanes, and A. Shleifer (2004), 'Do institutions cause growth?', Boston, MA: NBER Working Paper No. 10568.

Goldberg, V.P. (1976), 'Regulation and administered contracts', *Bell Journal of Economics*, 7 (Autumn): 426–48.

Goldberg, V.P. and J.R. Erickson (1982), 'Quantity and price adjustment in long-term contracts: a case study of petroleum coke', *Journal of Law and Economics*, 30: 369–98.

Golden, M.A. (2018), 'Corruption and the new institutional economics', in C. Menard and M. Shirley, eds., *A Research Agenda for New Institutional Economics*, Cheltenham, UK and Northampton, MA, USA: Edward Elgar: 171–7.

Golden, M.A. and P. Mahdavi (2015), 'Institutional foundations of political corruption', in J. Gandhi and R. Ruiz-Rufino, eds., *Routledge Handbook of Comparative Political Institutions*, Abingdon, UK and New York: Routledge: 404–20.

Gonzalez, C.G. (2009), 'Squatters, pirates, and entrepreneurs: is informality the solution to the urban housing crisis?', *University of Miami Inter-American Law Review*, **42** (2): 239–59.

Grafton, R.Q., D. Squires, and K.J. Fox (2000), 'Private property and economic efficiency: a study of a common-pool resource', *Journal of Law and Economics*, **43** (2): 679–714.

Granovetter, M. (1985), 'Economic action and social structure: the problem of embeddedness', *American Journal of Sociology*, **91** (3): 481–510.

Greif, A. (1993), 'Contract enforceability and economic institutions in early trade: the Maghribi traders', *American Economic Review*, **83** (3): 525–47.

Greif, A. (1994), 'Cultural beliefs and the organization of society: a historical and theoretical reflection on collectivist and individualist societies', *Journal of Political Economy*, **102** (5): 912–50.

Greif, A. (2005), 'Commitment, coercion, and markets: the nature and dynamics of institutions supporting exchange', in C. Menard and M.M. Shirley, eds., *Handbook of New Institutional Economics*, Dordrecht: Springer: 727–86.

Greif, A. (2006), *Institutions and the Path to the Modern Economy. Lessons from Medieval Trade*, Cambridge: Cambridge University Press.

Greif, A. and D.D. Laitin (2004), 'A theory of endogenous institutional change', *American Political Science Review*, **98** (4): 633–52.

Greif, A. and J. Mokyr (2017), 'Cognitive rules, institutions, and economic growth: Douglass North and beyond', *Journal of Institutional Economics*, **13** (1): 25–52.

Greif, A. and G. Tabellini (2017), 'The clan and the city: sustaining cooperation in China and Europe', *Journal of Comparative Economics*, **45** (1): 1–35.

Greif, A., P. Milgrom, and B. Weingast (1994), 'Coordination, commitment and enforcement. The case of merchant guild', *Journal of Political Economy*, **102** (4): 745–76.

Groenewegen, J., A. Spithoven, and A. van den Berg (2010), *Institutional Economics: An Introduction*, Houndmills, UK: Palgrave Macmillan.

Grossman, S. and O. Hart (1986), 'The costs and benefits of ownership: a theory of vertical and lateral integration', *Journal of Political Economy*, **94** (4): 691–719.

Guiso, L., P. Sapienza, and L. Zingales (2006), 'Does culture affect economic outcomes?', *Journal of Economic Perspectives*, **20** (2): 23–48.

Guriev, S. and D. Treisman (2015), 'How modern dictators survive: cooptation, censorship, propaganda, and repression', Centre for Economic Policy Research, London, Discussion Paper No. 10454.

Guriev, S. and D. Treisman (2019), 'Informational autocrats', *Journal of Economic Perspectives*, **33** (4): 100–27.

Hadfield, G.K. (2015), 'The many legal institutions that support contractual commitments', in C. Menard and M.M. Shirley, eds., *Handbook of New Institutional Economics*, Dordrecht: Springer: 175–204.

Haggard, S. and M.D. McCubbins (2001), 'Introduction: political institutions and the determinants of public policy', in S. Haggard and M.D. McCubbins, eds., *Presidents, Parliaments, and Policy*, New York: Cambridge University Press: 1–17.

Hahn, R. (2003), 'The economics of patent protection: policy implications from the literature', accessed on June 10, 2020 at SSRN: https://ssrn.com/abstract=467489.

Hamilton, J.W. (2016), 'Contamination at U.S. military bases: profiles and responses', *Stanford Environmental Journal*, **35** (2): 223–49.

Hardin, G. (1968), 'The tragedy of the commons', *Science*, **162** (3859): 1243–8.

Hart, O. (1995), *Firms, Contracts, and Financial Structure*, Oxford: Clarendon Press.

Hart, O. and J. Moore (1988), 'Incomplete contracts and renegotiations', *Econometrica*, **56** (4): 755–85.

Hart, O. and J. Moore (1990), 'Property rights and the nature of the firm', *Journal of Political Economy*, **98** (6): 1119–58.

Hart, O. and J. Moore (1999), 'Foundations of incomplete contracts', *Review of Economic Studies*, **66** (1): 115–38.

Hart, O. and J. Moore (2008), 'Contracts as reference points', *Quarterly Journal of Economics*, **123** (1): 1–48.

Hartwell, C.A. (2017), 'Determinants of property rights in Poland and Ukraine: the polity or politicians?', *Journal of Institutional Economics*, **13** (1): 133–60.

Henrich, J. (2016), *The Secret of our Success: How Culture Is Driving Human Evolution, Domesticating Our Species, and Making Us Smarter*, Princeton, NJ: Princeton University Press.

Henrich, J. (2020), *The WEIRDest People in the World. How the West Became Psychologically Peculiar and Particularly Prosperous*, New York: Farrar, Straus and Giroux.

Herrmann, B., C. Thöni, and S. Gächter (2008), 'Antisocial punishment across societies', *Science*, **319**: 1362–7.

Hodgson, G.M. (1989), 'Institutional economic theory: the old versus the new', *Review of Political Economy*, **1** (3): 249–69.

Hodgson, G.M. (1998), 'The approach of institutional economics', *Journal of Economic Literature*, **36** (1): 166–92.

Hodgson, G.M. (2014), 'On fuzzy frontiers and fragmented foundations: some reflections on the original and new institutional economics', *Journal of Institutional Economics*, **10** (4), 591–611.

Hodgson, G.M. (2015), *Conceptualizing Capitalism: Institutions, Evolution, Future*, Chicago, IL: University of Chicago Press.

Huang, Z., L. Li, G. Ma, and L.C. Xu (2017), 'Hayek, local information, and commanding heights: decentralizing state-owned enterprises in China', *American Economic Review*, **107** (8): 2455–78.

Huang, Z., J. Liu, G. Ma, and L.C. Xu (2020), 'The effects of privatization: evidence from a natural experiment', World Bank Policy Research Working Paper No. 9261.

IMF (International Monetary Fund) (2003), *World Economic Outlook, April 2003: Institutions and Growth*, Washington, DC: International Monetary Fund.

IMF (International Monetary Fund) (2020), 'State-owned enterprises: the other government', in *IMF Fiscal Monitor April 2020*, Chapter 3: 47–74, accessed on April 7, 2020 at https://www.imf.org/en/Publications/FM/Issues/2020/04/06/fiscal-monitor-april-2020.

Joskow, P. (1985), 'Vertical integration and long-term contracts: the case of coal-burning electric generating plants', *Journal of Law, Economics, and Organization*, **1** (1): 33–80.

Joskow, P. (1987), 'Contract duration and relationship-specific investment: empirical evidence from the coal market', *American Economic Review*, 77 (May): 168–85.

Joskow, P. (1988), 'Asset specificity and the structure of vertical relationships: empirical evidence', *Journal of Law, Economics, and Organization*, 4: 95–117.

Joskow, P. (1989), 'Regulatory failure, regulatory reform, and structural change in the electrical power industry', *Brookings Papers: Microeconomics 1989*: 125–208.

Joskow, P. (1991), 'The role of transaction cost economics in antitrust and public utility regulatory policies', *Journal of Law, Economics and Organization*, 7 (Spring): 253–83.

Joskow, P. (2002), 'Transaction costs economics, antitrust rules and remedies', *Journal of Law, Economics and Organization*, 18 (1): 95–116.

Joskow, P. (2005), 'Vertical integration', in C. Menard and M.M Shirley, eds., *The Handbook of New Institutional Economics*, Dordrecht: Springer: 316–48.

Joskow, P.L. and R.J. Noll (2013), 'Alfred E. Kahn, 1917–2010', *Review of Industrial Organization*, 42(2): 107–26.

Kaiser, K. and S. Wolters (2013), 'Fragile states, elites, and rents in the Democratic Republic of Congo (DRC)', in D.C. North, J.J. Wallis, S.B. Webb, and B.R. Weingast, eds., *In the Shadow of Violence. Politics, Economics and the Problems of Development*, New York: Cambridge University Press: 70–111.

Kamiński, A. (1975), 'Neo-serfdom in Poland-Lithuania', *Slavic Review*, 34 (2): 253–68.

Keefer, P. (2005), 'Democratization and clientelism: why are young democracies badly governed?', Washington, DC: World Bank Policy Research Working Paper 3594, May.

Keefer, P. (2011), 'Collective action, political parties and pro-development public policy', World Bank, Policy Research Working Paper Series 5676, accessed on July 10, 2020 at https://ideas.repec.org/p/wbk/wbrwps/5676.html.

Keefer, P. (2018), 'Collective action and government; still a mystery', in C. Menard and M.M. Shirley, eds., *A Research Agenda for New Institutional Economics*, Cheltenham, UK and Northampton, MA, USA: Edward Elgar: 9–19.

Keefer, P. and S. Khemani (2005), 'Democracies, public expenditures, and the poor: understanding political incentives for providing public services', *World Bank Research Observer*, 20 (1): 1–27.

Keefer, P. and D. Stasavage (2003), 'The limits of delegation: veto players, central bank independence, and the credibility of monetary policy', *The American Political Science Review*, 97 (3): 407–23.

Keefer, P. and R. Vlaicu (2007), 'Democracy, credibility, and clientelism', *The Journal of Law, Economics, and Organization*, 24 (2): 371–406.

Keefer, P., M. Espinoza, A. Espinoza, and R. Fort (2019), 'The impact of social ties and third-party enforcement on collective action and growth. Micro evidence from Peru', Inter-American Development Bank Working Paper No. IDB-WP-1061.

Kikeri, S., J. Nellis, and M.M. Shirley (1992), *Privatization: The Lessons of Experience*, Washington, DC: World Bank.

Kingston, C. and G. Caballero (2009), 'Comparing theories of institutional change', *Journal of Institutional Economics*, 5 (2): 151–80.

Kitch, E.W. (1983), 'The fire of truth: a remembrance of law and economics at Chicago, 1932–1970', *Journal of Law and Economics*, **26** (1): 163–233.

Klein, B. (1980), 'The borderlines of law and economic theory: transaction cost determinants of "unfair" contractual arrangements', *American Economic Review*, **70** (May): 356–62.

Klein, B. (1996), 'Why "hold-ups" occur: the self enforcing range of contractual relationships', *Economic Inquiry*, **34**: 444–63.

Klein, B. (2000a), 'The role of incomplete contracts in self-enforcing relationships', *Revue d'Economie Industrielle*, **92**: 67–80.

Klein, B. (2000b), 'Fisher-General Motors and the nature of the firm', *Journal of Law and Economics*, **43** (1): 105–41.

Klein, B. and K. Leffler (1981), 'The role of market forces in assuring contractual performance', *Journal of Political Economy*, **89**: 615–41.

Klein, B., R. Crawford, and A.A. Alchian (1978), 'Vertical integration, appropriable rents, and the competitive contracting process', *Journal of Law and Economics*, **21** (2): 297–326.

Klein, P. (2005), 'The make-or-buy decision: lessons from empirical studies', in C. Menard and M.M. Shirley, eds., *Handbook of New Institutional Economics*, Dordrecht: Springer: 435–64.

Knack, S. and P. Keefer (1995), 'Institutions and economic performance: cross-country tests using alternative institutional measures', *Economics and Politics*, **7** (3): 207–27.

Knack, S. and P. Keefer (1997), 'Does social capital have an economic payoff? A cross-country investigation', *The Quarterly Journal of Economics*, **112** (4): 1251–88.

Knight, F.H. (1921), *Risk, Uncertainty, and Profit*, Boston: Houghton-Mifflin.

Koopmans, T.C. (1947), 'Measurement without theory', *The Review of Economics and Statistics*, **29** (3): 161–72.

Kornhauser, L. and B. MacLeod (2013), 'Contracts between legal persons', in Robert Gibbons and John Roberts, eds., *Handbook of Organizational Economics*, Princeton, NJ: Princeton University Press: 918–57.

Kornhauser, L. and R. Mnookin (1979), 'Bargaining in the shadow of the law', *Yale Law Journal*, **88**: 950–97.

Krueger, A. (1990), 'The political economy of controls: American sugar', in M. Scott and D. Lal, eds., *Public Policy and Economic Development: Essays in Honor of Ian Little*, Oxford: Clarendon Press: 170–216.

Kunneke, R., C. Menard, and J. Groenewegen (2021), *Network Infrastructures: Technology Meets Institutions*, New York and Cambridge: Cambridge University Press.

La Porta, R., F. Lopez-de-Silanes, A. Shleifer, and R. Vishny (1997), 'Legal determinants of external finance', *Journal of Finance*, **52** (3): 1131–50.

La Porta, R., F. Lopez-de-Silanes, A. Shleifer, and R. Vishny (1998), 'Law and finance', *Journal of Political Economy*, **106** (6): 1113–55.

La Porta, R., F. Lopez-de-Silanes, A. Shleifer, and R. Vishny (1999), 'The quality of government', *Journal of Law, Economics and Organization*, **15** (1): 222–82.

La Porta, R., F. Lopez-de-Silanes, A. Shleifer, and R. Vishny (2000), 'Investor protection and corporate governance', *Journal of Financial Economics*, **58** (1–2): 3–27.

Laffont, J-J. and D. Martimort (2002), *The Theory of Incentives: The Principal-Agent Model*, Princeton, NJ: Princeton University Press.

Laffont, J-J. and J. Tirole (1993), *A Theory of Incentives in Procurement and Regulation*, Cambridge, MA: MIT Press.

Lafontaine, F. and M. Slade (2007), 'Vertical integration and firm boundaries: the evidence', *Journal of Economic Literature*, **45**: 629–85.

Lafontaine, F. and M. Slade (2013), 'Inter-firm contracts', in R. Gibbons and J. Roberts, eds., *Handbook of Organizational Economics*, Princeton: Princeton University Press: 958–1013.

Levi, M. (1988), *Of Rule and Revenue*, Berkeley and Los Angeles, CA: University of California Press.

Levi, M. (2000), 'When good defenses make good neighbors: a transaction cost approach to trust, the absence of trust and distrust', in C. Menard, ed., *Institutions, Contracts, and Organizations: Perspectives from New Institutional Economics*, Cheltenham, UK and Northampton, MA, USA: Edward Elgar: 137–57.

Levy, B. (2013), 'Seeking the elusive developmental knife edge: Zambia and Mozambique – a tale of two countries', in D.C. North, J.J. Wallis, S.B. Webb, and B.R. Weingast, eds., *In the Shadow of Violence. Politics, Economics, and the Problems of Development*, Cambridge: Cambridge University Press: 112–48.

Levy, B. and P.T. Spiller (1994), 'The institutional foundations of regulatory commitment: a comparative analysis of telecommunications regulation', *Journal of Law, Economics, and Organization*, **10** (2): 201–46.

Levy, B. and P.T. Spiller (1996), *Regulations, Institutions, and Commitment: Comparative Studies of Telecommunications*, Cambridge: Cambridge University Press.

Libecap, G.D. (1978), 'Economic variables and the development of the law: the case of western mineral rights', *The Journal of Economic History*, **38** (2): 34–58.

Libecap, G.D. (1998), 'Unitization', in P. Newman, ed., *New Palgrave Dictionary of Economics and the Law*, Vol. 3, New York: Macmillian: 641–3.

Libecap, G.D. (2008a), 'The tragedy of the commons: property rights and markets as solutions to resource and environmental problems', *Agricultural and Resource Economics*, **53** (1): 129–44.

Libecap, G.D. (2008b), 'Open-access losses and delay in the assignment of property rights', *Arizona Law Review*, **50** (2): 379–408.

Libecap, G.D. (2014), 'Addressing global environmental externalities: transaction cost considerations', *Journal of Economic Literature*, **52** (2): 424–79.

Libecap, G.D. (2018), 'Douglass C. North: transaction costs, property rights, and economics outcomes', NBER Working Paper 24585, accessed on April 7, 2020 at https://www.nber.org/papers/w24585.

Lo, D., M. Ghosh, and G. Zanarone (2020), 'Governing investments in inter-firm collaborations: the role of contracts', Working Paper, accessed on December 2, 2020 at https://www.researchgate.net/publication/341742029.

Long, C. (2018), 'The China experience: an institutional approach', in C. Menard and M.M. Shirley, eds., *A Research Agenda for New Institutional Economics*, Cheltenham, UK and Northampton, MA, USA: Edward Elgar: 135–42.

Long, C. and X. Zhang (2011), 'Cluster-based industrialization in China: financing and performance', *Journal of International Economics*, **84**: 112–23.

Lopes de Mendonça, F. and P. Furquim de Azevedo (2014), 'Independence of the judiciary: measuring the political bias of the Brazilian courts', Paper presented to the Annual Conference of the International Society for New Institutional Economics at Duke University, June 2014, accessed on July 3, 2020 at https://papers.sioe.org/durham.html.

Lü, X., M. Liu, and F. Li (2018), 'Policy coalition building in an authoritarian legislature: evidence from China's national assemblies', *Comparative Political Studies*, **53** (9): 1380–416.

Lubell, M. (2007), 'Familiarity breeds trust: collective action in a policy domain', *Journal of Politics*, **69** (1): 237–50.

Macaulay, S. (1963), 'Non-contractual relations in business: a preliminary study', *American Sociological Review*, **28** (1): 1–23.

Macchiavello, R. and A. Morjaria (2015), 'The value of relationships: evidence from a supply shock to Kenyan rose exports', *American Economic Review*, **105** (9): 2911–45.

Macher, J.T. and B.D. Richman (2008), 'Transaction cost economics: an assessment of empirical research in the social sciences', *Business and Politics*, **10** (1): 1–63.

Mackie, G. (1996), 'Ending footbinding and infibulation: a convention account', *American Sociological Review*, **61** (6): 999–1017.

MacLeod, B. and J. Malcolmson (1989), 'Implicit contracts, incentive compatibility, and involuntary unemployment', *Econometrica*, **57**: 447–80.

Macneil, I.R. (1974), 'The many futures of contracts', *Southern California Law Review*, **47**: 691–816.

Macneil, I.R. (1978), 'Contracts: adjustment of long-term economic relations under classical, neoclassical, and relational contract law', *Northwestern University Law Review*, **72** (6): 854–905.

Makadok, R. and R. Coff (2009), 'Both market and hierarchy: an incentive-systems theory of hybrid governance forms', *The Academy of Management Review*, **34** (2), 297–319.

Mandeville, B. (1732, reprinted 1988), *The Fable of the Bees, or Private Vices, Publick Benefits*, Indianapolis, IN: Liberty Press.

Masten, S.E. (1984), 'The organization of production: evidence from the aerospace industry', *Journal of Law and Economics*, **27** (October): 403–17.

Masten, S.E. (1988, reprinted 1991), 'A legal basis for the firm', in O.E. Williamson and S. Winter, eds., *The Nature of the Firm*, Oxford: Oxford University Press: 196–212.

Masten, S.E., J.W. Meehan, and E.A. Snyder (1991), 'The costs of organization', *Journal of Law, Economics, and Organization*, **7** (1): 1–25.

Matson, J., M. Tang, and S. Wynn (2012), 'Intellectual property and market power in the seed industry: the shifting foundations of our food system', University of Wisconsin Law School Government and Legislative Clinic, accessed on April 4, 2020 at https://papers.ssrn.com/abstract=2153098.

Maurer, S.M. and S. Scotchmer (2006), 'Open source software: the new intellectual property paradigm', NBER Working Paper No. 12148.

Mayer, K. and N. Argyres (2004), 'Learning to contract: evidence from the personal computer industry', *Organization Science*, **5**: 394–410.

McCloskey, D. (2006), *The Bourgeois Virtues: Ethics for an Age of Commerce*, Chicago, IL: University of Chicago Press.

McCloskey, D. (2010), *Bourgeois Dignity: Why Economics Can't Explain the Modern World*, Chicago, IL: University of Chicago Press.

McCloskey, D. (2016a), *Bourgeois Equality: How Ideas, Not Capital or Institutions, Enriched the World*, Chicago, IL: University of Chicago Press.

McCloskey, D. (2016b), 'Max U *versus* humanomics: a critique of neo-institutionalism', *Journal of Institutional Economics*, **12** (1), 1–27.

McCubbins, M.D. (2005), 'Legislative process and the mirroring principle', in C. Menard and M.M. Shirley, eds., *Handbook of New Institutional Economics*, Dordrecht: Springer: 91–122.

McCubbins, M.D., R.G. Noll, and B.R. Weingast (1987), 'Administrative procedures as instruments of political control', *Journal of Law, Economics, and Organization*, **3** (2): 243–77.

McCubbins, M.D., R.G. Noll, and B.R. Weingast (1989), 'Structure and process, politics and policy: administrative arrangements and the political control of agencies', *Virginia Law Review*, **75** (2): 431–82.

McMillan, J. and C. Woodruff (2000), 'Private order under dysfunctional public order', *University of Michigan Law Review*, **98** (8): 101–38.

Medema, S.G. (2020), 'The Coase theorem at sixty', *Journal of Economic Literature*, **58** (4): 1045–128.

Medina, L.F. (2013), 'The analytical foundations of collective action theory: a survey of some recent developments', *Annual Review of Political Science*, **16**: 259–83.

Megginson, W.L. (2017), 'Privatization, state capitalism, and state ownership of business in the 21st century', *Foundations and Trends in Finance*, **11** (1–2): 1–82.

Megginson, W.L. and J.M. Netter (2001), 'From state to market: a survey of empirical studies on privatization', *Journal of Economic Literature*, **39** (2): 321–89.

Meltzer, A.H. and S.F. Richard (1981), 'A rational theory of the size of government', *Journal of Political Economy*, **89** (5): 914–27.

Menard, C. (1996), 'On clusters, hybrids, and other strange forms: the case of the French poultry industry', *Journal of Institutional and Theoretical Economics*, **152** (1): 154–83.

Menard, C. (2004a), 'The economics of hybrid organizations', *Journal of Institutional and Theoretical Economics*, **160** (3): 345–76.

Menard, C., ed. (2004b), *The International Library of New Institutional Economics*, Cheltenham, UK and Northampton, MA, USA: Edward Elgar, 7 Volumes.

Menard, C. (2013a), 'Hybrid modes of organization. Alliances, joint ventures, networks, and other "strange" animals', in R. Gibbons and J. Roberts, eds., *The Handbook of Organizational Economics*, Princeton, NJ: Princeton University Press: 1066–108.

Menard, C. (2013b), 'Plural forms of organizations: where do we stand?', *Managerial and Decision Economics*, **34** (3–5): 124–39.

Menard, C. (2014), 'Embedding organizational arrangements: towards a general model', *Journal of Institutional Economics*, **10** (4): 567–89.

Menard, C. (2016), 'Ronald H. Coase and the economics of network infrastructure', in C. Menard and E. Bertrand, eds., *The Elgar Companion to Ronald H. Coase*, Cheltenham, UK and Northampton, MA, USA: Edward Elgar: 187–202.

Menard, C. (2017), 'Meso-institutions: the variety of regulatory arrangements in the water sector', *Utilities Policy*, **49** (December): 6–19.

Menard, C. (2018), 'Organization and governance in the agri-food sector: how can we capture their variety?', *Agribusiness: An International Journal*, **34** (1): 141–60.

Menard, C. and M. Ghertman, eds. (2009), *Regulation, Deregulation, Reregulation. An Institutional Perspective*, Cheltenham, UK and Northampton, MA, USA: Edward Elgar.

Menard, C. and M.M. Shirley (2005), *Handbook of New Institutional Economics*, Dordrecht: Springer.

Menard, C. and M.M. Shirley (2014), 'The contribution of Douglass North to New Institutional Economics', in S. Galiani and I. Sened, eds., *Institutions, Property Rights and Economic Growth: The Legacy of Douglass North*, New York: Cambridge University Press: 11–29.

Menard, C. and M.M. Shirley (2018), *A Research Agenda in New Institutional Economics*, Cheltenham, UK and Northampton, MA, USA: Edward Elgar.

Menard, C., P. Schnaider, and S. Saes (2018), 'Heterogeneity of plural forms: a revised transaction cost approach', *Managerial and Decision Economics*, **39**: 652–63.

Merrill, T. (2002), 'Introduction: the Demsetz thesis and the evolution of property rights', *The Journal of Legal Studies*, **31**(2): 331–8.

Milgrom, P., D.C. North, and B. Weingast (1989), 'The role of institutions in the revival of trade: the law merchant, private judges, and the Champagne fairs', *Economics and Politics*, **2**: 1–23.

Miller, G.J. (1992), *Managerial Dilemmas. The Political Economy of Hierarchy*, Cambridge and New York: Cambridge University Press.

Mintzberg, H. (1983), *Structure in Fives. Designing Effective Organizations*, Englewood Cliffs, NJ: Prentice-Hall.

Mittal, S. and B.R. Weingast (2010), 'Self-enforcing constitutions: with an application to democratic stability in America's first century', APSA 2010 Annual Meeting Paper, accessed on July 9, 2020 at https://ssrn.com/abstract=1643199.

Moe, T.M. (1984), 'The new economics of organization', *American Journal of Political Science*, **28** (4): 739–77.

Moe, T.M. (1990), 'Political institutions: the neglected side of the story', *Journal of Law, Economics, and Organization*, **6** (Special Issue 1990): 213–53.

Moe, T.M. (2013), 'Delegation, control, and the study of public bureaucracy', in R. Gibbons and J. Roberts, eds., *The Handbook of Organizational Economics*, Princeton, NJ and Oxford: Princeton University Press: 1148–81.

Moe, T.M. and M. Caldwell (1994), 'The institutional foundations of democratic government: a comparison of presidential and parliamentary systems', *Journal of Institutional and Theoretical Economics (JITE)*, **150** (1): 171–95.

Mokyr, J. (2002), *The Gifts of Athena: Historical Origins of the Knowledge Economy*, Princeton, NJ: Princeton University Press.

Mokyr, J. (2016, reprinted 2018), *A Culture of Growth: Origins of the Modern Economy*, Princeton, NJ: Princeton University Press.

Monteverde, K.C. and D.J. Teece (1982), 'Suppliers switching costs and vertical integration in the automobile industry', *Bell Journal of Economics*, **13** (1): 206–13.

Montinola, G.R. (2013), 'Change and continuity in a limited access order: the Philippines', in D.C. North, J.J. Wallis, S.B. Webb, and B.R. Weingast, eds. (2013), *In the Shadow of Violence. Politics, Economics, and the Problems of Development*, Cambridge: Cambridge University Press: 149–97.

Mueller, B. (2018), 'The coevolution of institutions and culture', in C. Menard and M. Shirley, eds., *A Research Agenda for New Institutional Economics*, Cheltenham, UK and Northampton, MA, USA: Edward Elgar: 153–61.

Mulherin, J.H. (1986), 'Complexity in long-term contracts: an analysis of natural gas contractual provisions', *Journal of Law, Economics, and Organization*, **2** (1): 105–17.

Musacchio, A. and S.G. Lazzarini (2014), *Reinventing State Capitalism: Leviathan in Business, Brazil, and Beyond*, Cambridge, MA: Harvard University Press.

Myerson, R. (2004), 'Justice, institutions, and multiple equilibria', *Chicago Journal of International Law*, **5** (1): 91–107.

Nee, V. and S. Opper (2012), *Capitalism from Below. Markets and Institutional Change in China*, Cambridge, MA and London: Harvard University Press.

Nelson, R.R. and S.G. Winter (1982), *An Evolutionary Theory of Economic Change*, Cambridge, MA: The Belknap Press of Harvard University.

Niehans, J. (1987), 'Transaction costs', in J. Eatwell, M. Milgate, and P. Newman, eds., *The New Palgrave: A Dictionary of Economics*, London: MacMillan. Vol. IV: 676–9.

Nobel, B. (2018), 'Authoritarian amendments: legislative institutions as intraexecutive constraints in post-Soviet Russia', *Comparative Political Studies*, **53** (9): 1417–54.

North, D.C. (1981), *Structure and Change in Economic History*, Cambridge: Cambridge University Press.

North, D.C. (1984), 'Government and the cost of exchange in history', *Journal of Economic History*, **44**: 255–64.

North, D.C. (1986), 'Sources of productivity in ocean shipping, 1600–1850', *The Journal of Political Economy*, **76** (5): 953–70.

North, D.C. (1987), 'Institutions, transaction costs and economic growth', *Economic Inquiry*, **25** (3): 419–28.

North, D.C. (1990a), *Institutions, Institutional Change and Economic Performance*, Cambridge: Cambridge University Press.

North, D.C. (1990b), 'A transaction cost theory of politics', *Journal of Theoretical Politics*, **2** (4): 355–67.

North, D.C. (1991), 'Institutions', *The Journal of Economic Perspectives*, **5** (1): 97–112.

North, D.C. (2005), *Understanding the Process of Economic Change*, Princeton, NJ: Princeton University Press.

North, D.C. and R.P. Thomas (1973, reprinted 1999), *The Rise of the Western World: A New Economic History*, Cambridge: Cambridge University Press.

North, D.C. and J.J. Wallis (1986), 'Measuring the transaction sector in the American economy, 1870–1970', in S.L. Engerman and R.E. Gallman, eds.,

Long-Term Factors in American Economic Growth, Chicago, IL: University of Chicago Press: 95–161.

North, D.C. and B.R. Weingast (1989), 'Constitutions and commitment: the evolution of institutions governing public choice in seventeenth-century England', *The Journal of Economic History*, **49** (4): 803–32.

North, D.C., W. Summerhill, and B.R. Weingast (2000), 'Order, disorder and economic change: Latin America vs. North America', in B. Bueno de Mesquita, and H. Root, eds., *Governing for Prosperity*, New Haven, CT: Yale University Press: 17–58.

North, D.C., J.J. Wallis, and B.R. Weingast (2009), *Violence and Social Orders: A Conceptual Framework for Interpreting Recorded Human History*, New York: Cambridge University Press.

North, D.C., J.J. Wallis, S.B. Webb, and B.R. Weingast, eds., (2013), *In the Shadow of Violence. Politics, Economics, and the Problems of Development*, Cambridge: Cambridge University Press.

Nunn, N. (2009), 'The importance of history for economic development', *Annual Review of Economics*, **1**: 65–92.

Olson, M. (1965), *The Logic of Collective Action: Public Goods and the Theory of Groups*, Cambridge, MA: Harvard University Press.

Olson, M. (1993), 'Dictatorship, democracy, and development', *American Political Science Review*, **87** (3): 567–76.

Ostrom, E. (1990), *Governing the Commons: The Evolution of Institutions for Collective Action*, Cambridge: Cambridge University Press.

Ostrom, E. (1996), 'Incentives, rules of the game, and development', in *Proceedings of the Annual Bank Conference on Development Economics 1995*, Washington, DC: World Bank: 207–34.

Ostrom, E. (2000), 'Collective action and the evolution of social norms', *Journal of Economic Perspectives*, **14** (3): 137–58.

Ostrom, E. (2005), 'Doing institutional analysis: digging deeper than markets and hierarchies', in C. Menard and M.M. Shirley, eds., *Handbook of New Institutional Economics*, Dordrecht: Springer: 819–45.

Ostrom, E. (2009), 'Beyond markets and states: polycentric governance of complex economic systems', *American Economic Review*, **100** (3): 641–72.

Ostrom, E. (2014), 'Do institutions for collective action evolve?', *Journal of Bioeconomics*, **16** (1): 3–30.

Ouchi, W.G. (1980), 'Markets, bureaucracies, and clans', *Administrative Science Quarterly*, **25**: 129–41.

Oxley, J. (1997), 'Appropriability hazards and governance in strategic alliances: a transaction cost approach', *Journal of Law, Economics and Organization*, **13** (2): 387–409.

Oxley, J. (1999), 'Institutional environment and the mechanism of governance: the impact of intellectual property protection on the structure of inter-firm alliances', *Journal of Economic Behavior and Organization*, **38** (3): 283–309.

Pande, R. and C. Udry (2005), 'Institutions and development: a view from below', Yale University, Economic Growth Center Discussion Paper No. 928.

Park, S.H. and Y. Luo (2001), '*Guanxi* and organizational dynamics: organizational networking in Chinese firms', *Strategic Management Journal*, **22**: 455–77.

Parker, D.P. (2018), 'Questions of property rights', in C. Menard and M.M. Shirley, eds., *A Research Agenda for New Institutional Economics*, Cheltenham, UK and Northampton, MA, USA: Edward Elgar: 111–18.

Parker, D.P. and B. Vadheim (2017), 'Resource cursed or policy cursed? US regulation of conflict minerals and violence in the Congo', *Journal of the Association of Environmental and Resource Economists*, **4** (1): 1–49.

Payne, G. (2001), 'Urban land tenure policy options: titles or rights?', *Habitat International*, **25** (3): 415–29.

Peltzman, S. (1989), 'The economic theory of regulation after a decade of deregulation', *Brookings Papers on Economic Activity*: 1–41.

Peng, M.W. and P.S. Heath (1996), 'The growth of the firm in planned economies in transition: institutions, organizations, and strategic choice', *The Academy of Management Review*, **21** (2): 492–528.

Persson, T. and G. Tabellini (2002), *Political Economics: Explaining Public Policy*, Cambridge, MA: MIT Press.

Pincus, S.C.A. and J.A. Robertson (2014), 'What really happened during the Glorious Revolution?', in S. Galiani and I. Sened, eds., *Institutions, Property Rights and Growth: The Legacy of Douglass North*, New York: Cambridge University Press: 192–222.

Posner, R.A. (1969), 'Natural monopoly and its regulation', *Stanford Law Review*, **21** (February): 548–643.

Potters, J. and R. Sloof (1996), 'Interest groups: a survey of empirical models that try to assess their influence', *European Journal of Political Economy*, **12** (3): 403–43.

Powell, W.W. and P.J. DiMaggio (1991), *The New Institutionalism in Organizational Analysis*, Chicago, IL: University of Chicago Press.

Prüfer, J. and P. Prüfer (2018), 'Data science for institutional and organizational economics', in C. Menard and M.M. Shirley, eds., *A Research Agenda for New Institutional Economics*, Cheltenham, UK and Northampton, MA, USA: Edward Elgar: 248–59.

Przeworski, A. (1991), *Democracy and the Market*, Cambridge: Cambridge University Press.

Qian, Y. and B.R. Weingast (1996), 'China's transition to markets: market-preserving federalism, Chinese style', *Journal of Policy Reform*, **1** (2): 149–85.

Razzaz, O.M. (1993), 'Examining property rights and investment in informal settlements: the case of Jordan', *Land Economics*, **69** (4): 341–55.

Reder, Melvin (1999), *Economics: The Culture of a Controversial Science*, Chicago, IL: University of Chicago Press.

Reuer, J.J. and S.V. Devarakonda (2016), 'Mechanisms of hybrid governance: administrative committees in non-equity alliances', *Academy of Management Journal*, **59** (2): 510–33.

Rodrik, D., A. Subramanian, and F. Trebbi (2004), 'Institutions rule: the primacy of institutions over geography and integration in economic development', *Journal of Economic Growth*, **9**: 131–65.

Rubin, P.H. (2005), 'Legal systems as frameworks for market exchange', in C. Menard and M.M. Shirley, eds., *Handbook of New Institutional Economics*, Dordrecht: Springer: 205–28.

Rutherford, M. (1994), *Institutions in Economics: The Old and the New Institutionalism*, Cambridge: Cambridge University Press.

Rutherford, M. (2001), 'Institutional economics: then and now', *Journal of Economic Perspectives*, **15** (3): 173–94.

Sachs, J. (2003), 'Institutions don't rule: direct effects of geography on per capita income', NBER Working Paper No. 9490, accessed on August 20, 2020 at http://www.nber.org/papers/w9490.

Savedoff, W.D. and P.T. Spiller (1999), *Spilled Water: Institutional Commitment in the Provision of Water Services*, Washington, DC: InterAmerican Development Bank.

Schimmelpfennig, D., C.E. Pray, and M. Brennan (2003), 'The impact of seed industry concentration on innovation: a study of U.S. biotech market leaders', accessed on April 5, 2020 at https://ssrn.com/abstract=365600.

Schotter, A. (1981), *The Economic Theory of Social Institutions*, Cambridge: Cambridge University Press.

Schwartz, A. (1992), 'Relational contracts in the courts: an analysis of incomplete agreements and judicial strategies', *Journal of Legal Studies*, **21**: 271–318.

Shelanski, H. and P. Klein (1995), 'Empirical research in transaction costs economics', *Journal of Law, Economics and Organization*, **11** (2): 335–61.

Shepsle, K.A. and B.R. Weingast (1981), 'Structure-induced equilibrium and legislative choice', *Public Choice*, **37** (3): 503–19.

Shepsle, K.A. and B.R. Weingast (1984), 'When do rules of procedure matter?', *Journal of Politics*, **46** (February): 206–21.

Shepsle, K.A. and B.R. Weingast (1987), 'The institutional foundations of committee power', *American Political Science Review*, **81** (March): 85–104.

Shirley, M.M. (1983), 'Managing state owned enterprises', Washington, DC: World Bank Staff Working Paper No. 577.

Shirley, M.M., ed. (2002), *Thirsting for Efficiency: The Economics and Politics of Urban Water System Reform*, Oxford: Elsevier Science B.V.

Shirley, M.M. (2008), *Institutions and Development*, Cheltenham, UK and Northampton, MA, USA: Edward Elgar.

Shirley, M.M. (2013), 'Battles lost and wars won: reflections on "The problem of social cost"', *Journal of Natural Resources Policy Research*, **5** (4): 243–7.

Shirley, M.M. and J. Nellis (1991), *Public Enterprise Reform: The Lessons of Experience*, Washington, DC: World Bank.

Shirley, M.M. and P. Walsh (2000), 'Public versus private ownership: the current state of the debate', Washington, DC: World Bank, Policy Research Working Paper 2420.

Shirley, M.M., L.C. Xu, and A.M. Zuluaga (2002), 'Reforming urban water supply: the case of Chile', in M.M. Shirley, ed., *Thirsting for Efficiency: The Economics and Politics of Urban Water System Reform*, Oxford, UK: Elsevier Science B.V.: 189–231.

Shirley, M.M., N. Wang, and C. Menard (2015), 'Ronald Coase's impact on economics', *Journal of Institutional Economics*, **11**: 227–44.

Siems, M. (2006), 'Legal origins', CBC Research Paper No. 0023, accessed on September 24, 2020 at SSRN: http://ssrn.com/abstract=879720.

Simison, E. and D. Ziblatt (2018), 'The power and limits of federalism', in C. Menard and M.M. Shirley, eds., *A Research Agenda for New Institutional*

Economics, Cheltenham, UK and Northampton, MA, USA: Edward Elgar: 27–33.

Simon, H.A. (1947, reprinted 1961), *Administrative Behavior*, New York: Macmillan.

Simon, H.A. (1951), 'A formal theory of the employment relationship', *Econometrica*, **19** (3): 293–305.

Simon, H.A. (1957), *Models of Man*, New York: Wiley.

Simon, H.A. (1978), 'Rationality as process and as product of thought', *American Economic Review*, **68** (2): 1–16.

Simon, H.A. (1979), 'Rational decision making in business organizations', *American Economic Review*, **69** (4): 493–513.

Skarbek, D. (2020), 'Qualitative research methods for institutional analysis', *Journal of Institutional Economics*, **16** (4): 429–31.

Smith, A. (1776, reprinted 1976), *An Inquiry into the Nature and Causes of The Wealth of Nations*, Oxford: Oxford University Press.

Spiller, P.T. (2009), 'An institutional theory of public contracts: regulatory implications', in C. Menard and M. Ghertman, eds., *Regulation, Deregulation, Reregulation. An Institutional Perspective*, Cheltenham, UK and Northampton, MA, USA: Edward Elgar: 45–66.

Spiller, P.T. (2010), 'Regulation: a transaction cost perspective', *California Management Review*, **52** (2): 147–58.

Spiller, P.T. and M. Tommasi (2005), 'The institutions of regulation', in C. Menard and M.M. Shirley, eds., *Handbook of New Institutional Economics*, Dordrecht: Springer: 515–43.

Spiller, P.T. and M. Tommasi (2007), *The Institutional Foundations of Public Policy in Argentina: A Transactions Cost Approach*, Cambridge: Cambridge University Press.

Stein, H. (2005), 'Intellectual property and genetically modified seeds: the United States, trade and the developing world', *Northwestern Journal of Technology and Intellectual Property*, **3** (2): 160–78.

Steven, F. (2018), *Law and Development. An Institutional Critique*, Cheltenham, UK and Northampton, MA, USA: Edward Elgar.

Stigler, G.J. (1966), *The Theory of Price*, 3rd edn, New York: Macmillan.

Stigler, G.J. (1971), 'The theory of economic regulation', *Bell Journal of Economics and Management Science*, **2** (1): 3–21.

Stigler, G.J. (1988), *Memoirs of an Unregulated Economist*, New York: Basic Books.

Stinchcombe, A. (1990), *Information and Organizations*, Berkeley, CA: University of California Press.

Stokes, S.C. (2005), 'Perverse accountability: a formal model of machine politics with evidence from Argentina', *American Political Science Review*, **99** (3): 315–25.

Sun, L. and P. Ho (2016), 'Formalizing informal homes, a bad idea: the credibility thesis applied to China's "extra-legal" housing', *Land Use Policy*, **79** (December): 891–901.

Tabellini, G. (2007), 'Institutions and culture', Università Bocconi, IGIER Working Paper No. 330.

Tadelis, S. and O.E. Williamson (2013), 'Transaction cost economics', in R. Gibbons and J. Roberts, eds., *The Handbook of Organizational Economics*, Princeton, NJ: Princeton University Press: 159–89.

Teorell, J. (2018), 'Measuring institutions: what we do not know', in C. Menard and M.M. Shirley, eds., *A Research Agenda for New Institutional Economics*, Cheltenham, UK and Northampton, MA, USA: Edward Elgar: 241–7.

Tirole, J. (1999), 'Incomplete contracts: where do we stand?', *Econometrica*, **67** (4): 741–82.

Trebilcock, M. and P-E. Veel (2008), 'Property rights and development: the contingent case for formalization', *University of Pennsylvania Journal of International Law*, **30** (2): 397–481.

Turvani, M. (1997), 'Illegal markets and new institutional economics', in C. Menard, ed., *Transaction Cost Economics*, Cheltenham, UK and Lyme, NH, USA: Edward Elgar: 127–48.

Vahabi, M., P. Batifoulier, and N. Da Silva (2020), 'The political economy of revolution and institutional change: the elite and mass revolutions', *Revue d'Économie Politique*, **130** (6): 855–89.

Van Laerhoven, F. and E. Ostrom (2007), 'Traditions and trends in the study of the commons', *International Journal of the Commons*, **1** (1): 3–28.

Varian, H.R. (1992), *Microeconomic Analysis* 3rd edn, Hoboken, NJ: Wiley.

Voigt, S. (2008), 'The economic effects of judicial accountability: cross-country evidence', *European Journal of Law and Economics*, **25** (2): 95–123.

Voigt, S. (2018), 'Internal institutions: the major unknowns in institutional economics', in C. Menard and M.M. Shirley, eds., *A Research Agenda for New Institutional Economics*, Cheltenham, UK and Northampton, MA, USA: Edward Elgar: 145–52.

Voigt, S. (2019), *Institutional Economics. An Introduction*, Cambridge: Cambridge University Press.

Voigt, S., J. Gutmann, and L.P. Field (2015), 'Economic growth and judicial independence, a dozen years on: cross-country evidence using an updated set of indicators', *European Journal of Political Economy*, **38** (June): 197–211.

Wei, S-J, Z. Xie, and X. Zhang (2017), 'From "Made in China" to "Innovated in China": necessity, prospect, and challenges', *Journal of Economic Perspectives*, **31** (1): 49–70.

Weingast, B.R. (1989), 'The political institutions of representative government: legislatures', *Journal of Institutional and Theoretical Economics (JITE)*, **145** (4): 693–703.

Weingast, B.R. (1993), 'Constitutions as governance structures: the political foundations of secure markets', *Journal of Institutional and Theoretical Economics (JITE)*, **149** (1): 286–311.

Weingast, B.R. (1995), 'The economic role of political institutions: market-preserving federalism and economic development', *Journal of Law, Economics and Organization*, **11** (1): 1–31.

Weingast, B.R. (1997), 'The political foundations of democracy and the rule of law', *American Political Science Review*, **91** (2): 245–63.

Weingast, B.R. (2005), 'The performance and stability of federalism: an institutional perspective', in C. Menard and M.M. Shirley, eds., *Handbook of New Institutional Economics*, Dordrecht: Springer: 149–72.

Weingast, B.R. (2007), 'Second generation fiscal federalism: implications for decentralized democratic governance and economic development', accessed on July 10, 2020 at https://ssrn.com/abstract=1153440.

Weingast, B.R. and W.J. Marshall (1988), 'The industrial organization of Congress; or, why legislatures, like firms, are not organized as markets', *Journal of Political Economy*, **96** (1): 132–58.

Weingast, B.R. and M.J. Moran (1983), 'Bureaucratic discretion or congressional control: regulatory policy making by the Federal Trade Commission', *Journal of Political Economy*, **91** (5): 765–800.

Wernerfelt, B. (1984), 'A resource-based view of the firm', *Strategic Management Journal*, **5** (2): 171–80.

Whinston, M. (2001), 'Assessing property rights and transaction-cost theories of the firm', *American Economic Review*, **91** (2): 184–8.

Williamson, O.E. (1971), 'The vertical integration of production: market failure considerations', *American Economic Review*, **61** (May): 112–23.

Williamson, O.E. (1975), *Markets and Hierarchies: Analysis and Antitrust Implications. A Study in the Economics of Internal Organization*, New York: Free Press.

Williamson, O.E. (1976), 'Franchise bidding for natural monopolies – in general and with respect to CATV', *The Bell Journal of Economics*, **7** (1): 73–104.

Williamson, O.E. (1979), 'Transaction cost economics: the governance of contractual relations', *Journal of Law and Economics*, **22** (2): 233–61.

Williamson, O.E. (1985a), *The Economic Institutions of Capitalism*, New York: Free Press.

Williamson, O.E. (1985b), 'Assessing contract', *Journal of Law, Economics and Organization*, **1**: 177–208.

Williamson, O.E. (1991), 'Economic institutions: spontaneous and intentional governance', *Journal of Law, Economics, and Organization*, **7**: 159–87.

Williamson, O.E. (1993), 'Calculativeness, trust, and economic organization', *Journal of Law and Economics*, **36** (1): 453–86.

Williamson, O.E. (1996), *The Mechanisms of Governance*, New York and Oxford: Oxford University Press.

Williamson, O.E. (2000), 'The New Institutional Economics: taking stock/looking ahead', *Journal of Economic Literature*, **37** (3): 595–613.

Williamson, O.E. (2002), 'The lens of contract: private ordering', *American Economic Review*, **92** (2): 438–43.

Williamson, O.E. (2005), 'Transaction cost economics', in C. Menard and M.M. Shirley, eds., *Handbook of New Institutional Economics*, Dordrecht: Springer: 41–65.

Williamson, O.E. (2010), 'Transaction cost economics: the natural progression', *American Economic Review*, **100**: 673–90. Revised version of Nobel Prize Lecture.

World Bank (1995), *Bureaucrats in Business*, New York: Oxford University Press.

Xu, C. (2011), 'The fundamental institutions of China's reform and development', *Journal of Economic Literature*, **49** (4): 1076–151.

Xu, C. (2015), 'China's political-economic institutions and development', *Cato Journal*, **35** (3): 525–48.

Yalcintas, A. (2010), 'The "Coase Theorem" vs. Coase Theorem proper: how an error emerged and why it remained uncorrected so long', MPRA Paper No. 37936, accessed on February 1, 2013 at http://mpra.ub.uni-muenchen.de/37936.

Yao, Y. and M. Zhang (2015), 'Subnational leaders and economic growth: evidence from Chinese cities', *Journal of Economic Growth*, **20** (4): 405–36.

Zak, P.J. and S. Knack (2001), 'Trust and growth', *Economic Journal*, **111** (470): 295–321.

Zanarone, G. (2013), 'Contract adaptation under legal constraints', *Journal of Law, Economics, and Organization*, **29**: 799–834.

Zanarone, G., D. Lo, and M. Ghosh (2020), 'Governing investment in inter-firm collaborations: the role of contracts', Working Paper, May.

Zhang, F. (2018), *The Institutional Evolution of China. Government as Market*, Cheltenham, UK and Northampton, MA, USA: Edward Elgar.

Zhang, W. (2019), 'The China model view is factually false', *Journal of Chinese Economic and Business Studies*, **17** (3): 287–311.

Zucker, L.G. (1988), *Institutional Patterns and Organizations*, Cambridge, MA: Ballinger.

Index

Titles in the **Elgar Advanced Introductions** series include: